At Close
Quarters

At Close Quarters

A CEO's Guide to Navigating the Unanticipated Government Investigation and Regulatory Enforcement Action: *Internal Investigations, Best Practices, Mistake Avoidance and the Corporate Compliance Value Proposition*

Allan J Sullivan *with* Heber C. Maughan CPA & Linda Joy Sullivan CPA

ISBN: 0692971890
ISBN 13: 9780692971895
Library of Congress Control Number: 2017916344
Third River Publishing, New York, NY

Foreword

This work, as a legal writing, is not particularly ambitious. You will not find in the following pages a single citation to legal authority, there are no footnotes or appendices, and there will not be space devoted to abstract discussions of complex legal concepts.

But it is far from superficial. Everything in this book is grounded in the law and is based on decades of experience helping numerous clients who have had to deal with prosecutors, agents and government officials who suspect or, worse, who have already concluded that a business – or one or more of its owners, executives, managers, employees, suppliers or distributors – has done something very wrong. Something criminal even.

We set out here to provide the business that has rarely if ever been involved in a government investigation or regulatory enforcement action a simply-written guide outlining some of the most common events – and attending processes and protocols – that follow the commencement of a law enforcement investigation. While it identifies a number of best practices and suggests possible alternative responses to the government's efforts, our aim ultimately is simply to inform and demystify a process that many find intimidating and frightening.

In the process, we suggest the utility of the early adoption of a strategic orientation that in the first instance emphasizes the avoidance of the sorts of mistakes made by many organizations that suddenly and unexpectedly find themselves under investigation. Because the legal and practical consequences flowing from any given government investigation are usually not predictable at the very outset of the government's work, we have found that some clients mentally telescope ahead to a hypothetical array of really bad possible outcomes: indictments, arrests, fines, imprisonment and forfeitures. Management of a public company in particular will begin immediately to worry about not just how to manage the looming media relations nightmare but how best to respond to the inevitable expressions of investor angst or outrage that are soon to follow. Thoughts often soon stray to other far less intuitive consequences – long-term company valuation losses, possible earnings restatements, the loss of customers, employee layoffs, law suits, ruined careers and defections of essential personnel. The danger of projecting ahead too far -- and too negatively -- is the risk that management may lose sight of the imperative to attend carefully to the very important tasks and demands that will be most immediately at hand at the very beginning of the ordeal. "Taking care of business" in these circumstances requires great focus and deliberateness by management in fashioning critical early responses to the sudden and unexpected threat posed by the government's interest in the enterprise.

The same caution applies to management's orientation during later stages of the government's efforts. Investigations and regulatory enforcement actions usually follow a fairly predictable course. Many important decision points will present themselves as the investigation matures. There is almost always time carefully to work through different strategic approaches to how the business will engage both with the government and with important constituents of the enterprise. Experience has shown the critical importance of preventing this otherwise manageable process from turning into a long and escalating series of mistake-ridden crises. Calm and deliberateness will always be the order of the day. This writing offers practical recommendations and suggestions directed towards the avoidance of oft-recurring management foot faults -- errors that can prove problematic when, at the end of the process, the business gets to the point of exploring acceptable resolutions with the government.

We do all this in a way designed to educate and inform without belaboring the reader with unnecessary resort to legal jargon or lawyer-to-lawyer "*inside baseball.*" The tone is deliberately conversational. The intended audience is the business professional needing to better understand and wrestle with a unique business problem, and one that will present itself in different forms over the following months, such as how to anticipate the execution of a possible search warrant or "*dawn raid,*" deal with government requests for informal witness interviews, respond to investigative subpoenas, prepare managers for grand jury appearances and provide employees with requested legal help. Most importantly, we set out early in this work to educate the reader as to how best to get a handle on the all-important facts that most likely led to the government's interest in the business in the first instance – facts that will ultimately drive important decision-making by the company at each and every step of the way.

Our approach is to mimic what a good lawyer would explain in plain language to a sophisticated lay client about what are sometimes hard to understand processes. The book does not need to be read in its entirety or sequentially. It has been written to make the topics addressed here quickly accessible without having to read preceding chapters for fear that important preliminary concepts have been overlooked.

We hope, among other things, to show that, by promptly obtaining the assistance of a lawyer and supporting forensic professionals schooled in government investigations, a company can both greatly help avoid early mistakes and increase its ability later to mitigate the array of possible bad outcomes that may lie ahead. We also, by informing the reader of the typical processes associated with government investigations and enforcement actions, aspire to promote appropriately-calibrated discussions between lawyer and client during each phase of the government's efforts.

Perhaps most importantly, we seek ultimately to convince the reader that management's genuine embrace of robust preventive measures -- through promotion of a true "*culture of compliance*" within the organization and by investments in not so hard to design and implement compliance infrastructure -- can pay enormous dividends when, at the end of the process, the government makes its decisions about prosecutions, fines, imprisonment and other much more benign, and yet often quite attainable, outcomes.

⌒

DISCLAIMER: *This Guide is not intended to serve as a comprehensive delineation and examination of the many potential legal issues that can arise in the context of the government's launch, or potential launch, of a criminal investigation, prosecution or regulatory enforcement action. It is not offered as legal advice and the information contained in this Guide should not be relied upon as such.*

The laws, rules and procedures relating to criminal and regulatory processes differ from jurisdiction to jurisdiction, from agency to agency and from federal to state, and this Guide does not attempt to call out or reconcile those many differences. Rather, the Guide outlines certain processes common to most investigations, wherever conducted, largely from the orientation of federal practice and procedure.

The provision of legal advice typically requires an attorney's full understanding of individual facts and all of the surrounding circumstances, followed by a tailored application of the law unique to the jurisdiction whose laws control. In other words, the appropriate legal response to any particular issue or predicament cannot be found simply upon a lay reading of a general introduction to a subject such as is presented in the following pages. If advice concerning a specific matter or other legal assistance is needed, the service of a competent professional should be sought.

Table of Contents

Introduction

The receipt of a grand jury subpoena or investigative demand, or of other news suggesting that federal or state law enforcement agents and prosecutors have developed an interest in a business, invariably causes great alarm. At times, particularly where the business is aware of the basis for the government's interest, the alarm is fully warranted – federal law enforcement officials have been increasingly aggressive in prosecuting and punishing business crimes, and even the collateral consequences to a company or to an executive that has become a *"subject"* or *"target"* of an investigation can be many. At other times, the level of alarm is more the function of the unknown. Owners and managers of compliance-conscious, law-abiding businesses typically have no significant experience that will help them understand whether the interest of law enforcement should be a cause of real concern or whether the worst-case outcomes that spring to mind are mostly imagined. While management will invariably turn to their in-house counsel or trusted outside attorney to answer the flood of questions that such events usually prompt, the reality is that the *law enforcement* legal terrain is alien to many of the most seasoned lawyers.

Devising effective management responses to the initiation and later progression of any criminal or regulatory investigation requires the making of very difficult and often subjective judgments. Management is thus best advised promptly to enlist the assistance of a legal professional and, if at all possible, counsel having significant *white-collar* criminal defense and corporate compliance experience, not only to guide the company through the investigation but to avoid errors that can affect the perceptions that law enforcement officials form about a company and its managers. The adverse appearances that can flow from early management missteps are often hard to shake and they can significantly – and negatively – affect the outcome of an investigation or enforcement action.

The following materials provide a summary exposition of the law enforcement landscape that businesses and their managers must sometimes traverse. Our identification and description of fundamental investigative protocols and standards is based predominantly on *federal* criminal practice and procedure. Federal prosecutors and the federal judiciary have long taken the lead in developing *best practice* in the areas we address below. The use of a federal criminal law and procedure lens allows us to address concepts that are largely common to the work of most investigatory authorities throughout the United States – prosecutors, regulators and law enforcement agencies alike. We approach the subjects addressed in the six chapters below on the uncontroversial premise that government investigations, no matter their jurisdictional grounding, generally proceed within a common framework and along fairly predictable timelines. Still, the reader is cautioned that the laws, rules and practices followed by authorities in individual states may differ from some of the processes and protocols described below. Also, some regulatory agencies on the federal level have detailed written guidelines governing how they conduct their investigations, initiate regulatory enforcement processes and resolve their cases. Resort must always ultimately be had then to the local laws of individual jurisdictions or to the specific rules and processes applicable to the regulatory agency involved.

We start at Chapter I addressing at some length the critical importance, at the first sign of possible government trouble, of conducting an effective *triage* of the situation at hand and thereafter promptly embarking upon as error-free an *internal investigation* as can be had to get to the root of the government's interest. We devote particular attention to identifying the important decision points that will present themselves to management at the outset of enforcement activity, and there are many. The point of Chapter I is largely to underscore the need for management to make smart decisions very early on. Hurried reactions, including internal and external expressions of hostility to the government's work, can cause great harm. Deliberateness is critical. Early and careful internal fact-finding is indispensable. There is usually abundant time to make intelligent choices about how best to launch the internal reviews and investigations that are necessary to inform decision-making throughout the process ahead and we address in this Chapter a number of best practices that sophisticated business organizations employ when launching and conducting internal investigations.

At Chapter II, we suggest ways management can best prepare for and respond to a government decision to execute the highly intrusive – and business disrupting – search warrant. Many business people believe the search warrant to be the stuff of grimier investigations, used by the "*cops*" to unravel complicated murder mysteries or to dismantle drug distribution rings or racketeering organizations. The reality is that law enforcement authorities in the United States have long used this tool when investigating "*paper*" crimes, as the element of surprise and lack of pre-warning reduces the risk that documents critical to a case will disappear or that computer drives and laptops will be cleansed. In Europe and Asia too, the so-called "*dawn raid*" has been employed commonly at the outset of even the most complicated investigations of antitrust, intellectual property and other business crimes. While the search warrant surprise factor creates an opportunity for the *government* to collect evidence that might otherwise evade authorities, it creates great risk to the *business* subject to the search -- particularly, the risk that local managers on the scene will, in the interest of protecting themselves or the company, make mistakes during the search that may later prove costly and the risk that the company will publicly overreact to the event and cause for itself lasting perception problems. In this Chapter we focus on best practices senior management should consider when called upon to manage this most exigent of law enforcement encounters.

In Chapters III and IV we discuss the bread-and-butter stage of any *white-collar* investigation: the issuance of subpoenas for documents and records, the interview of employees and managers and the summonsing of witnesses to appear and testify before a grand jury or other investigative body. Here, there is usually abundant time for careful attention to how best to respond to such standard requests for physical evidence and testimony so as to ensure that the company remains perceived by the government as fully committed to cooperating with the investigators. Risks remain, however. Sometimes government requests for access to witnesses may come without warning (and may not even be directed to the company at all) and there is always the possibility that, unless potential evidence is secured early on, things will disappear before the government gets there. Nothing can be worse for a company or individual who has become a subject or target of an investigation than to have the government conclude that efforts were taken to obstruct its investigation. These Chapters focus on prudent precautions to ensure that this more routine phase of a government investigation is navigated without adverse incident.

Chapter V is dedicated to a discussion of the considerations government officials take into account when determining whether to charge a company or its management and, when that happens, the possible array of sanctions business entities and individuals may face. Focus on the *"end game"* – and close and early attention by management to what company counsel will be trying to achieve in his or her discussions with the government at the beginning, middle and end of the process – enormously informs how the company should go about defending its interests throughout the investigation. In order to appropriately set the table for a discussion of the range of possible bad outcomes ahead for any company under investigation – and of the sometimes-limited discretion afforded to a prosecutor to make choices between them – not insignificant early attention in this Chapter is devoted to describing the charging and sentencing processes employed by the government and the courts. Then, beyond identifying the worst of the worst-case outcomes (prison, fines, forfeitures, *etc.*), we address a few of the *"happy endings"* that may follow a lengthy investigation of a business, such as the government's decision to decline prosecution entirely or the employment of specially sanctioned agreements (known as *"deferred prosecution agreements"* and *"non-prosecution agreements"*) that federal prosecutors have been permitted to use to conditionally shut down business-related investigations.

We conclude at Chapter VI, importantly, with consideration of some of the many easy-to-implement and cost-effective prevention and risk reduction measures that can help businesses avoid the more draconian of the bad outcomes that might follow a government investigation. It is today the expectation of regulators and investigators that companies of any significant size or complexity will have in place compliance protocols and processes designed to avoid and detect improper conduct. This Chapter explains why, even without this expectation, fostering a robust compliance environment is nothing short of a prudent risk management strategy that should pay dividends far beyond the avoidance or mitigation of government sanction should something go wrong.

We cover a lot of ground and so, consistent with the goals of this work, the materials below serve only as a "*primer*" of sorts to help frame and inform a company's discussions with its counsel and ultimately with the government. In each chapter, we approach the subject at hand pragmatically, by posing an imaginary scenario, followed by treatment of the range of critical legal and strategic issues that management often must grapple with when navigating the unhappy fact that a business and its people have become the subjects of a government investigation. Of course, as must be said here, the scenarios we paint below are entirely fictional, and no connection should be made to real persons or events. The lessons to be drawn by the fact patterns, on the other hand, are very real.

Chapter 1

A Frequent Companion to the Government Investigation: The *Internal* Investigation

Businesses have long relied upon the *internal investigation* to discover the scope of suspected financial frauds, accounting irregularities and other business misconduct. The internal investigation is an important corporate risk assessment and mitigation tool, critical to achieving and maintaining of the sort of robust *"culture of compliance"* expected both by the government and by the investment community in which any credible allegation of material misconduct will be investigated by the business thoroughly and in a timely fashion.

While inquiry into more routine or less serious matters may be handled informally (*e.g.*, by reviews or audits conducted by a compliance officer, an internal auditor or in-house counsel), the current regulatory and law enforcement environment is not particularly forgiving of companies that under-react to evidence of material internal misconduct. Boards of directors, senior management and in-house counsel increasingly face situations calling for the launch of a vigorous internal investigation involving at least the assistance of, if not direction by, outside professionals. Those professionals may include accountants and others able to help conduct forensic examinations. But they also increasingly involve, in a leadership capacity, outside counsel experienced in not only conducting such investigations but in negotiating with law enforcement personnel and regulators.

These internal investigations are best commenced at the first sign of serious trouble, whether the government is aware or not of the cause for concern. Potentially costly and disruptive, the decision by a business to launch a truly independent and thorough fact investigation, and to follow it with appropriate remediation, can go far in allaying the concerns of regulators, prosecutors and shareholders about the company's tolerance of improper conduct. In addition, the commencement of an internal investigation can serve as a critical first step in assisting management deal with the potentially catastrophic consequences of law enforcement actions or regulatory interventions, stave off costly litigation, and manage the perception of the company by the public, shareholders, employees and other important constituents. It may also mean the difference in later shareholder litigation against individual board members premised upon their alleged failure to act prudently in the discharge of their fiduciary obligations when faced with troubling allegations of employee or management misconduct.

There are, as will be discussed throughout this Chapter, many very early and critical judgment calls that must be made by management whenever any material government trouble presents itself. First among those will be whether even to launch an internal investigation. Questions influencing that decision will abound: *Is the allegation credible? Does it suggest the commission of unlawful acts? How pervasive and complex are the alleged misdeeds? Are the underlying facts likely to become known, either within the company or externally? If the allegation is substantiated, will there be any significant financial consequence or will there be a financial reporting requirement?* And, if an investigation is to be commenced, the company will next need to determine the scope of the review and how it is to be led and staffed.

The active assistance of outside counsel is highly advisable in making even these very early decisions, particularly where there is the possibility that the government will in fact involve itself. Adoption of a *"wait and see"* approach can lead to disastrous lost opportunities that may otherwise have enabled the company, through counsel, to better frame early discussions with the government. Indeed, in the right circumstances, and particularly where a business has demonstrated an early and unequivocal commitment to investigate a matter thoroughly, the government has been known to stand down and defer its work pending the company's completion of its internal reviews. The value of achieving such an early concession from the government – or even in simply setting the right tone with outside investigators who may be investigating along a parallel track – can be immeasurable.

The early detection of trouble is likewise critical. It cannot be emphasized enough that businesses need not only be ever-watchful for signs of employee misconduct but to respond promptly when it seems to have occurred. Important leads will come from any of a number of sources. Employee complaints or calls to "*compliance hotlines*" must be carefully scrutinized; credible information brought to the company by vendors or suppliers should be appropriately escalated; suspicious information and even rumors of improprieties uncovered during the internal audit process should always be pursued.

In addition, it is important that particularly timely and aggressive response be had to more open manifestations of problems: a news article; the launch of a government audit; the receipt of an investigative demand issued by a regulator; cause to suspect the existence of a still-secret civil "*whistleblower*" complaint; shareholder litigation or the receipt of an attorney demand letter; and overt law enforcement activities that appear to concern the business and even the markets in which it operates. Management must, the best it can, pursue any *red flags*, to include even the most unsubstantiated word of informal law enforcement interviews of third parties with whom a company does business, the issuance of grand jury subpoenas to competitors or suppliers, or the execution of a search warrant involving a participant in the company's relevant market.

A Hypothetical -- When Signs of Trouble First Appear

Consider, for purposes of the discussion below, the following scenario:

A little more than three years ago your company, a national, publicly–traded medical laboratory testing concern, acquired a company whose principal source of revenues was gen-etic or "molecular" testing. The acquired company had a large network of semi-independent "distributors" and service representatives that worked with hospitals, clinics and psychiatric practice groups to process a variety of pre-symptomatic screenings for hereditary mental illnesses. Shortly before the acquisition, the molecular lab company – Real Genetics, Inc. – landed what promised to be an extremely lucrative contract with the Veteran's Administration to conduct tests to gauge through genetic markers possible adverse reactions to medications used to treat depression and PTSD. The acquisition represented for your company a venture into an entirely new field – not only had your company no prior experience with molecular testing, but it had never directly contracted with the Veteran's Administration or, for that matter, with any other federal government entity.

The molecular testing company became, after its merger with your company, the nucleus of a new "Genetics Division" largely run by the management team of Real Genetics Inc. at its west coast headquarters 2,500 miles away from your principal offices. Disturbingly, during most of the initial post-acquisition period, Division management appeared openly resistant to the efforts of your company to centralize management systems and internal controls. Your internal auditors, IT professionals and financial and accounting professionals had battled geographic and institutional barriers to fully integrating the new Genetics Division's audit and financial reporting programs. Integration was largely advanced through attrition of Genetics Division senior personnel, the replacement of a few key Genetics Division managers whose responsibilities were assumed at your east coast corporate headquarters, and the promotion and transfer two months ago of the original founder of Real Genetics, Inc. to an executive management position at HQ (as well as his appointment to a position on the Company's Board of Directors and the Board's Audit Committee). Still, three years after the acquisition, the work around integrating the west coast operations was far from complete.

Recently, a middle level manager in your Genetics Division reported to your national Director of Compliance — requesting confidential treatment — that the Division had 12 months earlier received two VA Office of Inspector General ("VA-OIG") document requests. Although the Genetics Division was accustomed to periodic requests for information from the OIG of the Medicare authorities (the Department of Health and Human Services ("HHS-OIG")), these two VA requests appeared, according to the Genetics Division source, to be of considerable concern to the Genetics Division's CFO – a Real Genetics management holdover – and had apparently prompted a series of closed–door meetings and "worried looks" when the issue had come up at a staff meeting soon after the requests arrived. One of the requests seemed to focus on highly technical molecular testing protocols and the division's compliance with testing documentation requirements spelled out in the VA procurement contract. The second request more ominously called for the production of records that suggested the possibility that there had been billing "up coding" and "unbundling" which, if widespread, would have substantially – and possibly illegally – increased the Division's per-test federal reimbursement under not only the VA contract, but across its entire business, to include business lines funded by the federal Medicare and Medicaid programs.

Unlike the more routine HHS-OIG audit requests received by the Genetics Division over the last three years, the VA-OIG's requests had curiously never been forwarded to your company's Legal Department. Rather, the Genetics Division CFO had apparently gathered and delivered requested documents through the Division without assistance from HQ Legal. Your Compliance Director reported that a recent discrete follow up inquiry he had made to a trusted member of Genetics' finance group revealed that no one at the Genetics Division had since heard anything further from the VA-OIG. For all intents and purposes, the matter appeared dead. In fact, relations between the Genetics Division and the VA were excellent. Additional substantial – and very lucrative – procurement contracts were under negotiation with the VA and there existed no concrete evidence that the government had determined the existence of any specific documentation or reimbursement irregularities.

Because the Genetics Division's profits over the last three years had greatly bolstered otherwise sluggish financial results at your company, any significant coding fraud or government program reimbursement issues would inevitably be deemed material and, at a minimum, if made public, would create unease amongst investment analysts who had for some time suggested that your company's stock was overpriced. Those analysts had noted, among other things, high management compensation levels, including bonuses and perquisites exceeding those customary in the industry. Lavish expenditures for (entirely legal) high profile marketing and promotional events had also, in recent months, been the subject of industry media reports. To make matters worse, your Legal Department advised that if there was in fact a billing and reimbursement problem at the Division, significant risk existed that any federal Medicare program "exclusion," or federal procurement contract "debarment," consequence would extend to the entire company.

At a closed-door meeting of half a dozen senior managers this morning, two of your colleagues expressed very strongly the sentiment that the company should "let sleeping dogs lie," and even forego any informal internal review of the situation, at least until some positive indication existed that the government was actually in receipt of concrete evidence of internal misconduct. Concern was expressed that, no matter how discrete the review, word would get out around the company, and then to shareholders, that "we had a compliance problem 'out west.'" While you are less bothered about quantifying and returning to the government any improperly obtained VA, Medicare and Medicaid payments (as the law seemed to require), you deeply suspect that any investigation into the root cause of the billing issue might reveal not only intentional and fraudulent overbilling but other financial irregularities, including certain possible improper revenue recognition practices that had been whispered about since the acquisition three years ago.

Hesitancy by management to escalate an issue to problem status before its time is natural. It is complicated enough to run a business. Prematurely adding to the mix the need to attend to an amorphous, ill-defined allegation that may never "*have legs*" only makes more difficult achieving the seemingly more pressing short-term fiscal year operational and financial goals of the company. Taking pause is a valid instinct. But deciding not to go to a physician to avoid news of some feared malady is no way to live either. More facts are needed. Unfortunately, the early decision-making process around *"what to do next"* when faced with vague suggestions of wrong-doing can often be complicated.

On the one hand, failure promptly to get to the bottom of suspicious transactions or practices can later fuel government perceptions that senior management had long had actual knowledge of the irregularities and determined it best to wait to address them in the hope they would go undetected. Such perceptions amongst government investigators, once formed, are very hard to shake and can lead to the unfortunate expansion of a government investigation in search of other potential areas of institutional misconduct. On the other hand, a full-blown internal investigation might result in the discovery of conduct that would never have otherwise been revealed. In addition, knowledge within the company of even the launch of an internal investigation of any significance may, once public, lead to the opening by the government of its own criminal investigation or regulatory inquiries, and might also prompt negative media attention, affecting the price of a company's stock. The company will be mindful as well of the adverse consequence of an investigation on employee morale and upon the ability of senior management to avoid time and energy-consuming distractions from the imperatives of the day-to-day business of the company.

Ultimately, the company will most likely be told by its counsel that any credible allegation of significant misconduct needs to be investigated fully, in order to maintain internal accountability, to preserve the integrity of the company's compliance efforts, and to avoid individual liability of the company's directors based upon a failure to investigate internal misconduct in discharge of the Board's fiduciary obligations. It is imperative, counsel will advise, that the company work to avoid any possible perception by the government that management simply decided to hunker down and circle the wagons. But counsel will also advise that, if the investigation is appropriately structured, led and staffed, there is a more than reasonable prospect that the results of the internal investigation can be kept entirely confidential within the company.

Consider the most immediate *"process"* questions that might occur to members of a company's executive team when considering the launch of an internal investigation:

Who really owns the *decision* to investigate? If there is a decision formally to investigate a matter internally, who should *manage and oversee* it for the company? The Board? Management?

How best should the company staff and structure the investigation? Does it matter who does the actual investigating?

What will be the role, if any, of outside counsel? Of in-house counsel?

Is there any possibility, however remote, of complicity by C-level management in the activity to be investigated? Is there need to wall-off anyone from involvement in the investigation?

What will be the day-to-day role or involvement of management during the investigation? Who ought to be involved and receive reports about its progress?

What specifically should the employees and managers who inevitably become aware of the existence of the investigation be advised?

Is it expected that the company will be revealing the results of the investigation to the government? Are there affirmative self-reporting obligations? Or might the company qualify for benefits under an amnesty or "*voluntary disclosure*" program if misconduct is promptly disclosed?

Should the company be working towards preparation of a final "*report*" of investigation? Or is it better not to create written reports at all regarding the progression of and conclusions reached during an inquiry?

Can the company in fact keep the investigation entirely confidential?

Conducting an Effective Internal Investigation

The internal investigation is an extremely flexible device. It can be as formal or informal as the company chooses. It can be staffed entirely at the company's discretion. Its scope can be predetermined, and later expanded or contracted, entirely at company will. It can be reported to third parties. Or it can be conducted in a way, with some planning, that affords the results of it the status of a "*privilege*," and the protection of legal confidentiality, to such an extent that no one – not even a court – can later compel production of witness interviews or other written reports of investigation.

Sequentially below, we address: (1) how one approaches the early *"triage"* necessary to inform decisions about how best to move forward; (2) factors that ought to guide the decision to proceed and later inform the scope of the investigation; (3) who within or outside the business can or should be responsible for the actual conduct of the investigation; (4) the appropriate functions of management during the inquiry, including the management of internal and external communications; and (5) how best to approach the gathering of documents and witness statements.

The Importance of the Initial "Triage"

Upon the receipt of the stray and unanticipated allegation of internal wrongdoing, the instinct of most companies will be to dispatch an auditor, the compliance officer, or some mid-level manager to make a quick assessment of the facts. That's appropriate. Internal investigations can be costly and disruptive and not every allegation can be made the subject of an investigation assisted or led by outside professionals. But if the allegation or other initial indications suggest the involvement of high level managers, the commission of criminal acts or any material financial irregularities, this initial *"quick peek"* needs to be done very thoughtfully. While discussions among senior management as to the company's next steps will need to be particularly deliberate and well-informed, the initial fact-finding needs to be done deftly. Documents should be gathered and reviewed promptly and quietly. And, for reasons we set out below, if employees are talked to during any such non-lawyer-involved reconnaissance exercise, no substantially verbatim written statements or detailed summaries should be created. Written reports back to executive management or to the Board must likewise be circumspect and avoid the communication of definitive factual determinations.

This initial *triage* effort, when completed, is going to result in at least a preliminary finding landing somewhere along the continuum ranging from the good news that the allegations are entirely without foundation; to the relief-producing conclusion that the allegations are relatively insignificant and merit only modest additional investigation or remediation; to the worrisome realization that there are indeed troubling questions of such materiality to merit further formal investigation; to the really bad news that *"it's time to batten down the hatches"* as some inappropriate or unlawful conduct occurred that requires the company to get ready to defend and protect itself the best it can. A lot depends on making this call correctly. Misreading and incorrectly minimizing the severity of an allegation can have significant negative consequences.

We submit that serious consideration should be given to involving the company's attorneys in this early *triage* activity more often than not -- and particularly to do so whenever other than routine or trivial allegations of misconduct have been made. There are two important reasons for this.

Conducting a Legally Privileged and Confidential "First Look."

First, the early involvement of counsel may ensure that these preliminary inquiries and initial deliberations about *next steps* are themselves done discreetly and confidentially, and within the protection of the attorney-client privilege. Because it is an important topic that will be referenced throughout the following chapters, a few words are necessary here about the operation of the attorney-client privilege.

If a company's lawyer – or someone acting at the express direction of the lawyer – speaks confidentially to people within the company in order to gather facts intended to inform that lawyer's giving of legal advice, the communication is considered privileged and will remain strictly confidential as to anyone outside the company (provided no one later waives that privilege by breaching confidentiality). The same holds true for reports and analyses shared by the lawyer to the company's management. The policy underpinning of the *"legal confidentiality"* deemed to attend to a lawyer's conversations with employees, and to the lawyer's subsequent reports or discussions with a business client about the law and the facts learned by the lawyer from company witnesses, is the encouragement of early and candid discussions between counsel and client regarding the company's legal obligations with respect to circumstances threatening possible injury or liability exposure to the company. Through the privilege the law favors and promotes the early resort to counsel to help a business work though the resolution of knotty legal issues.

Beyond the attorney-client privilege, the law also recognizes that, where a lawyer writes a memorandum reflecting his or her conclusions or mental impressions about the gravity or credibility of allegations, the writings will in most instances also be protected as confidential by a somewhat lesser privilege extended to attorney "*work product.*" Here, too, as a matter of policy, the law seeks to encourage lawyers to thoroughly and candidly memorialize their legal impressions and conclusions so as to better assure that appropriate legal advice will be given to the client. Allowing an adversary or the government to obtain the often-subjective assessments of a lawyer as to the facts and the law applicable to a particular controversy or allegation would, it is thought, effectively discourage and chill the work of the lawyer necessary to ensure that disputes are efficiently resolved and that remediation, when that is appropriate, promptly occurs.

Importantly, the application of either privilege does not mean that the *facts* or *information* learned by the lawyer ever becomes protected from later discovery. But, properly protected, the lawyer's confidential internal conversations with the client about those facts and his or her own legal assessments of the situation are. Management can hear from the lawyer a candid analysis and recommendations without fear that the government will later discover what the lawyer reported.

Consider the scenario wherein a company chooses early on to defer participation of its lawyers and instead directs that the initial *triage* and questioning of employees be done by a mid-level operations, audit or financial manager without the involvement of counsel. No privilege attaches. Reports by the manager back to senior or executive management and the initial strictly-internal discussions as to what next to do will likewise not be considered legally confidential. The very first subpoena issued during a later government investigation (or even one issued in a private civil suit) relating to the matter will require the production of the manager's interview notes or email reports to higher-ups reflecting what could be a damning condemnation by a line employee of a senior member of company's management. However, if the manager had been instructed *by counsel* to conduct the preliminary interviews under counsel's supervision in order to assist counsel in advising management as to next steps, the notes and interview report are likely to be considered done by the manager as the lawyer's *"agent"* under the umbrella of the privilege – the report will remain as confidential and immune from later production as if done and prepared directly by counsel.

One can see, then, the usefulness of having an early conversation with company counsel whenever a credible allegation of material wrong-doing surfaces, and to have that discussion before even the most informal of inquiries is conducted. Indeed, having counsel lead the *triage* exercise itself may provide the company maximum flexibility in determining whether or not the allegation will ever subsequently to be disclosed to company outsiders. This does not mean to suggest that counsel will be used in order to *"hide the ball"* from the government. But, there are always going to be very difficult decisions to be made by a company as to how much of *any* investigation should be disclosed whether counsel is involved or not.

A decision not to fully disclose to the government the details or results of an internal investigation is often entirely prudent, legally appropriate and fully justified by factors having nothing whatever to do with a desire to hide information from the government. For example, because an early understanding of the facts based on the initial work done in an investigation is not infrequently overtaken by knowledge of facts later unearthed, disclosures of preliminary results – particularly those that seemingly exonerate the business or a manager – may be imprudent. Early interviews of witnesses by lawyers and non-lawyers alike, uninformed by extensive document reviews and the accounts of other witnesses, can easily result in the inadvertent preparation of an incomplete or inaccurate description of what actually happened or of what was told by a particular witness to the investigator. In addition, a decision to limit dissemination of the results of investigative efforts to the government may be required to reduce the risk of a later claim that the attorney-client privilege was *"waived"* by the disclosure, a finding that could later lead to required additional disclosures to persons outside the government who have an interest in using the information adversely against the company (*e.g.*, plaintiff's counsel in class action shareholder litigation).

Yet still, in other cases, the business may simply wish to deal with its own misconduct internally and quietly, through effective remedial measures not involving affirmative disclosures to the government. Not infrequently – in the view of many commentators – has a *"voluntary disclosure"* by a company to the government contributed to government enforcement decisions that fail to fully reflect a company's good faith in reporting the misdeeds of employees that may never have otherwise become known to the government.

Accordingly, use of counsel to help make these early factual assessments, and even later, to conduct and lead a fuller investigation, can give the business a number of diverse options in terms of what ultimately should be disclosed, if anything, to the government and in what form and when.

Providing Decision-Makers with Appropriate Advice as to Next Steps.

Here is a second, and in our view, more important, reason why early consultation with counsel is important:

Most of the important *triage* work that will go into the decision whether to launch a comprehensive internal investigation in the first instance and, if so, how to define its scope, how to staff it and how to resolve early process issues, involves at some level the application of facts to the law. In other words, deciding how a company should respond to troubling allegations of misconduct is usually driven by legal assessments that really ought to involve counsel.

What are those questions? We suggest that the answers to the following routinely presented questions will much influence the determination of what next ought to be done:

* If the allegations are substantiated, what is the potential for adverse regulatory action against the company? How significant is the company's regulatory, civil and criminal exposure?
* Is there in the circumstances an affirmative legal duty to develop evidence and self-report to the government? Would a failure quickly to report result in loss of an opportunity by the company to participate

in a regulatory *"amnesty"* or *"voluntary disclosure"* corporate mitigation program?

* How likely is the government to act on the information known once (and if) it learns of it? Does the subject matter implicate a law enforcement priority program? Is it criminal? Is there any history of the government's appetite for investigating matters such as these with other companies?

* Is the allegation or controversy known publicly and how likely is it to become public? How likely is it that even discrete early and entirely internal inquiries might become known throughout the company? To the government?

* Could the conduct at issue lead to the company's disbarment or exclusion from government programs? Might it affect an existing government contract?

* Could the conduct actually lead to the prosecution of employees? Who are the potential *"subjects"* of the investigation? How high in the organization are they?

* What is the potential, once revealed that the conduct at issue will result in civil litigation and expose the company to damages?

* Could a failure to investigate lead to later civil liability of the part of members of the Board of Directors?

* What is the potential that documents, emails or other important evidence will be discarded?

* Are there privacy and employment law considerations that will impede a prompt and thorough investigation?

* Will it be necessary to obtain evidence from foreign sources and are there special cross-border employee privacy rules that may come into play when seeking to obtain information from employees located outside the United States?

* Is there an obligation to report the allegation to an insurer under a Directors & Officers or General Liability policy?

* How long will it likely take to conclude an appropriately-scoped investigation?

* What will be the cost to the company of an internal investigation if external professionals (counsel, forensic accountants and technical experts) are required to lead or conduct it?
* Is there a possibility that a restatement of income will be required?
* What will be the effect of the allegations, if substantiated, on management's required certifications of its financial statements?
* What disclosure to outside auditors – and eventually investors – might be required? If publicly traded, is the company prepared to appropriately involve its Audit Committee in the exercise? Should the investigation be structured to the exclusion of management?
* Are the allegations the likely result of a whistleblowing complaint? Is there the possibility that there already exists a filed but secret federal *qui tam* action?
* What effect will a failure appropriately to respond have on the integrity of an existing compliance program?
* What is the likelihood that existing audit or compliance systems are deficient and in need of repair?
* What is, ultimately, the potential corporate liability for the wholly unauthorized misdeeds of its employees?

There is, then, substantial justification, and often *need*, during a company's early response to any material allegation of internal wrong-doing for early consultation with counsel. As we said above, it is important to get the early calls right. The government can be easily influenced, positively and negatively, by how a company reacts and what it does in response to its receipt of material allegations of internal misconduct.

Determining the Necessity for, Goals of, Risks in and the Scope of the Internal Investigation

While erring on the side of investigating is the most prudent course for the company forced to grapple with the consequences of the errant ways, ill-motivated or not, of its employees and of those with whom the organization does business, there are numerous risk-benefit considerations that must be taken into account in deciding whether to launch the larger effort and in defining the objectives of the investigation.

The decision-making *"matrix"* touches, we submit, four factors: (a) obligation; (b) benefit; (c) risk; and (d) scope. We address each in turn.

The "Obligation" to Conduct an Internal Investigation.

Nowhere is it written that a business is required legally to engage in the often painful and costly self-assessment and self-evaluation process inherent in any thorough internal investigation. Consider, though, the following legal (and moral) sources of such an *obligation*:

* A corporation, and members of its Board of Directors, have a general duty to deal with internal wrong-doing and to *"fix"* problems known to the company. Further, members of the management of public companies have enhanced disclosure and certification obligations post-Sarbanes-Oxley and post-Dodd Frank. There is understood to be an affirmative obligation to assess the financial impact of suspected misconduct and to report it to shareholders.

* Board members have increasingly been saddled with legal accountability for corporate misdeeds. Ultimately, the Board and its Audit Committee have fiduciary and at times statutory obligations to act affirmatively – and promptly – in the face of possible corporate misconduct.

* Prudence dictates that management and the Board, faced with the prospect of litigation, with the potential diminution of stock prices and with a possible regulatory intervention upon a public revelation of wrongdoing, must position themselves ahead of the public and governmental perception curve so that the impact of any eventual disclosure can be anticipated and minimized.

* The public, shareholders and regulators, following the many corporate financial scandals and prosecutions that have been launched in

the last 20 years, simply demand that every business be compliance conscious. Conducting an internal investigation may well be required simply as part of the cost of maintaining a genuine and robust corporate compliance environment.

* Insurers who issue Directors & Officer and General Liability insurance policies may by contract require prompt investigation and disclosure of events triggering coverage.

* In highly-regulated industries, there may exist (by statute, regulation or government contract) self-reporting obligations that cannot be avoided without adverse consequence by a course of corporate "*deliberate ignorance.*" Rules exist, for example, requiring affirmative disclosure and the return of government payments known to be improper and requiring notifications relating to data breaches or threats to the environment or public health.

"Benefits" to be Gained by Initiating a Thoughtful Internal Investigation.

Rather than think of the issue in terms of whether the circumstances *require* the commencement of an investigation, it is usually a much more productive exercise to factor in the advantages and *benefits* the company can glean from moving promptly and affirmatively to address a negative fact pattern.

Perhaps most significant is the potential that, by aggressively confronting a scenario likely eventually to capture the attention of regulators and law enforcement, the company can create an opportunity to convince the government that it ought to defer the commencement, or limit the scope, of any government investigative work pending the conclusion of the company's own investigation. Convincing the government to "*stand down*" and let the company take a first look and report the results of its own internal review can avoid the huge disruptions normally associated with a government investigation of a business.

Achieving this result may only come at a significant price, however. The company may be required, in order to obtain such a deferral or limitation of the government's independent efforts, to agree that the results (and even the particulars) of the company's internal investigation will be fully shared with law enforcement. Although gone are the days when the government would affirmatively demand production by a company of attorney-client privileged materials as the price for the receipt of leniency (an issue we deal with in Chapter V below), the government's agreement to defer entirely its investigation may be premised on the company's explicit and unequivocal commitment that it will liberally share all of its investigation materials (and results), good and bad, with the government. Moreover, early discussion with the government and pledges of cooperation designed to avoid or defer a largely disruptive government investigation might lead the government to expect that the unearthing of evidence of wrong-doing will result in immediate dismissals of otherwise valuable (and rehabilitated, in the eyes of the business) employees or managers or to insist upon other forms of remediation the company would in other circumstances wish to debate.

Despite the likelihood that the government will in most cases ultimately decide not to defer its investigation, but to pursue its own simultaneous, and parallel, inquiries, benefits can be realized from the company's decision to continue vigorously to investigate along-side the government. Prompt interview and document gathering exercises can put the company in a position to feed information to the government well earlier than the government would have acquired it on its own, further advancing the commitment that the company made to cooperate fully and in good faith. A thorough parallel internal investigation may permit the company itself to assess much earlier the potential complicity of insiders, allowing management more effectively to undertake damage control measures. The government might also come to rely on the company's disclosures as an important investigative resource, giving management some greater participation in the government's decision-making as to the scope and direction of its investigation, as well as permitting the company to exercise greater control over what gets voluntarily disclosed, when and how. A company's parallel investigation, when undertaken in a genuine spirit of cooperation, may also help prevent later government procurement disbarment or exclusion proceedings, or the imposition of civil money penalties, should misconduct short of the commission of criminal offenses be discovered. In the event criminal conduct is unearthed, moreover, the fact of self-policing and self-disclosures during a parallel investigation will almost invariably mitigate the consequences to the company should wrong-doing be unearthed, an issue we take up at length in Chapter V.

Other more collateral (but important) benefits can be derived from a company's prompt understanding of the parameters of a problem that has captured the government's full attention. An early and thorough investigation will often:

* Better arm civil counsel in anticipating or responding to litigation, including shareholder suits; will permit counsel to preserve important evidence and testimony, as well as to better prepare prospective witnesses; and it may serve to stave off (by early intervention and remedial measures undertaken by the company), claims for punitive damages or other extraordinary remedies based upon allegations that evidence of wrong-doing was ignored.
* Assist public relations personnel in mitigating the effects of public disclosures likely to lead to investor concerns.
* Send a clear signal throughout the company that there will be internal accountability for corporate misdeeds.
* Unearth flaws or weaknesses in the company's legal compliance and audit systems.
* Put the company in a posture that might deter entirely the filing of shareholder suits or that will discourage the initiation of False Claims Act lawsuits.

Assessing Downside Risk.

What, then, are the potential *downside consequences* of a decision to conduct an internal investigation? Might they outweigh the benefits?

The sheer cost and disruptions inherent in conducting an internal investigation can be significant, as can be the effect on employee or management morale. If conducted by outside counsel previously unfamiliar with your business, the learning curve – travelled during what can be a particular stressful episode in the company's history – can be tremendously upending. It is often difficult for employees to understand the role of these external lawyers for the company who show up asking hard and sometimes accusatory questions. And, external investigative "*teams*" usually are that – teams of more than one lawyer, investigator, accountant, *et al.* Done right, these investigations can be very costly. Absent effective management, they can also drag on indeterminately.

Another potential risk: Once a truly-independent internal investigation is started, management may eventually lose control of the situation and later be faced with making difficult decisions it would rather not have been required to make. It will be hard for the company not to terminate a valued member of its management team in the face of a conclusion by its lawyers that the manager was reckless or even complicit in wrongdoing, no matter how confidentially the finding is communicated.

Certainly, one can also imagine a situation where a company, having discovered preliminary evidence of fraud or other misconduct, initiates an investigation, the existence of which becomes known publicly, itself prompting a regulatory or law enforcement investigation that might never have otherwise been commenced. Knowledge outside the company of even the existence of an internal investigation might prompt press inquiries, adverse media coverage, and the incumbent circling of plaintiff's securities or class action counsel, sensing an opportunity for litigation and a lucrative settlement.

Similarly, there have been occasions where a company's efforts in promptly initiating an investigation and making disclosures to the government have not only failed to result in hoped-for leniency but have resulted in the government's affirmative use of voluntarily disclosed facts *against* the company when negotiating a final disposition or in sentencing the corporation or one or more of its employees. Those things happen – there will be times where negative "*political*" influences or the government's "*public perception*" concerns overcome all effort by a repentant company (and even a company that has undergone a top to bottom housecleaning) to capitalize on its present good faith and honest dealings. While experience tells us that the government ordinarily works hard to reward good behavior and genuine efforts at remediation, much of what the government strives to do in its priority white-collar enforcement programs is to make a clear example of offenders so as to affect the maximum deterrence of similar bad behavior by other businesses. Not everyone who has committed an offense will get investigated. The government will at times determine that a particular business needs simply to be made an example of despite prompt remediation – with harsh result – in order to demonstrate to others that truly bad things can happen to entities that break the law.

Determining the Scope of the Inquiry.

Sometimes it will be extremely tempting, then, for a company just to stand down and wait and see what happens. Yet, for all of the disruption, inconvenience, risk and cost, it is almost always in the best interest of a business to initiate an investigation, to determine for itself, as quickly as it can, the degree of its exposure and the scope of the collateral problems the company faces so that prudent, well-informed decisions can be made and made early to minimize the downside consequences. At a minimum, an early but complete assessment of the facts at issue will better assist counsel in advising the Board of Directors as to what it ought to consider doing in response. Further, as suggested earlier, obtaining information early-on may lead to a greater ability to manage the often-unwieldy consequences of a public controversy or scandal once it becomes public. Assuming an *"ostrich"* approach, or a path of *"deliberate ignorance,"* can lead to disastrous consequences – not the least of which is loss of control or influence over the direction and timing of an investigation that may eventually be completely taken over by hostile outsiders who have concluded that the company is seeking to evade responsibility for the bad conduct of its employees.

What, then, the *scope* of the internal investigation? Artificial limitations must be avoided. Conditions designed to assure management control over its progress will almost certainly be misperceived. Imagine in our *Genetics Division* hypothetical dispatching a team to investigate, but with a quietly-delivered side instruction that the team must limit the inquiry to precise technical coding questions and with strict instruction to communicate only verbally about the matter.

It is, of course, appropriate for management to help define the scope of the work, to later monitor the conduct of the investigation as well as to make ultimate decisions as to material next steps as the investigation develops. Management is well-advised, however, to assume that regulators or law enforcement will eventually learn of the particulars of meetings in which the parameters of an investigation have been discussed and deliberated within the company. Any appearance that management determined to undertake a superficial self-assessment for "*window-dressing*" purposes will always play very poorly. The better course is to guard against such perceptions by designing an investigation that is truly independent and by letting the investigation largely play its course. If management and the Board are committed to the exercise, the independence and breadth of the investigation can be memorialized and ultimately disclosed to the government with a genuine prospect of positive impact.

Who Conducts the Investigation?

Staffing the investigation is another important early decision. What will be the composition of the investigative team? The day-to-day role and involvement of management during the course of the investigation will be addressed in the next section. Here we focus on the company's options in terms of selecting the individual or entity primarily responsible for actually conducting the investigation – that is, gathering evidence, interviewing witnesses and reporting on the results.

How the company assembles an investigative team to examine allegations of material wrongdoing should never become just a matter of cost, or a determination of who is available to do the work. The decision ought to be guided, in the first instance, by consideration of the very *triage* factors we discussed above. The company needs deliberately to assess what is at stake and who will be the most likely outside entities (regulators, prosecutors, shareholders, media, *etc.*) that will be assessing how well management responded to the circumstances prompting the investigation. As we have suggested, how a company decides to staff the effort itself is often the subject of interest to the government in gauging the genuineness of the effort.

Several additional pragmatic also have to be considered: the desirability of using counsel to lead the investigation, so as to ensure the ability of management to control the extent of later disclosures of the results of the investigation; the need to maintain the integrity of the investigation by insulating the effort from inappropriate influences of members of management having a stake in the outcome; the importance of preserving the all-important appearance of independence of the investigating team; and, of course, the need to contain cost and internal disruption.

We outline below four separate staffing scenarios, involving the use of various internal and external forensic and audit professionals, compliance personnel, investigators and lawyers.

Internal Non-Attorney Staffing: Compliance Officer, Audit Staff and/or Human Resources Personnel.

As acknowledged at the outset of this Chapter, there will certainly be times, particularly when dealing with routine, lower-exposure allegations, where management will appropriately choose to have its internal compliance, audit or HR staff conduct an investigation and report the results directly to senior management.

Companies often, in fact, have on staff competent, highly experienced and well-trained non-legal professionals that management can trust to conduct internal inquiries thoroughly and with independence. Yet, this strictly *"internal"* approach has limitations and ought to be avoided if there is a possibility that the issue at hand may later generate public or government scrutiny. As we have addressed in some detail above, so staffed the results of the investigation, and interview notes generated during its course, will not ordinarily be protected from later compelled disclosure in litigation as they would when a privileged effort is undertaken by lawyers and those who work for them. In addition, the personnel tasked with conducting the investigation may have either been involved in or contributed in some way to the controversy (through affirmative act, oversight, failure to discover the misconduct or initial inaction upon learning of it); the personnel may have an actual reporting line obligation to potentially complicit managers; and there will always be the perception by outsiders, no matter how ill-founded, that an internal investigator is susceptible to influence by senior management or that the internal investigator may be influenced not to make adverse findings by either an instinct for self-preservation or an interest in career-advancement.

Avoidance of these latter perception issues are particularly critical when the company anticipates that it may later be required to convince a prosecutor that the company acted promptly and aggressively to unearth evidence of internal misconduct. If in fact the company wishes to be in a position to convince the government to avoid, defer or limit the scope of what could otherwise be an enormously disruptive and costly government-led investigation, its chances of prevailing in that effort will be diminished if the team assembled is entirely internal or comprised of relatively lower-level personnel.

The unfortunate reality is that some prosecutors will be immediately skeptical of the results of any purely internal inquiry due to concerns about its lack of independence. The U.S. Department of Justice has in years past published widely-disseminated memoranda criticizing what it perceived as a strategy employed by some companies of launching an internal investigative effort as part of a commitment of full cooperation when the investigative effort actually undertaken (and the remediation that followed) was but a form of "*window dressing*," launched primarily for appearance purposes. While it is not inappropriate to use existing, in-place resources to conduct internal investigations, management must be mindful of the motives that agents and prosecutors might attribute to management if it is perceived that the investigation has been lightly or inappropriately staffed by insiders.

The Use of In-House Counsel.

It is because of these sorts of perception issues that the tasking of in-house counsel with lead responsibility for an internal investigation (in other than routine settings) is also not ordinarily advisable. In-house counsel, no matter how competent, conscientious and diligent, may suffer many of the perceived limitations burdening the compliance officer or internal auditor – a lack of true independence, potential involvement directly or indirectly in the events leading to the controversy (including by giving, or not giving, legal advice regarding the matters at issue before they became the subject of the investigation), self-interest in not being critical of senior management, *etc.*

Also, one of the main benefits of the use of counsel to conduct or lead the investigation – the applicability of the attorney client privilege – may be only illusory when the attorney is a member of a company's "*in-house*" legal staff. Because in-house counsel often serve management as business advisors, separate and apart from providing purely legal advice, a later challenge during civil litigation to the company's invocation of the privilege to shield the results of an investigation and communications concerning "*remediation*" efforts may be much more difficult to turn back. A court may eventually find, for example, that counsel's involvement was not so much in a legal capacity (where the privilege attaches) as it was to help manage the situation from a business standpoint (where the privilege does not attach). If in-house counsel is asked to conduct the internal review, or to lead an internal investigative team, counsel must scrupulously and routinely document that he or she was acting in a legal, and not a business advisor, capacity.

Still, involvement and assumption by in-house counsel of an investigative leadership role is better than relegating the job entirely to the company's compliance team, no matter how good that team is. As we have addressed above, many issues – including process questions – will arise having legal implications. While in-house corporate counsel are not typically schooled in conducting internal investigations and have limited experience negotiating with law enforcement, in-house counsel can effectively and materially contribute to any corporate investigation.

The Retention of Outside Counsel.
It should not by this point be a surprise to read here that, in today's highly-charged regulatory and litigation environment, where government perceptions

are often all–important, management frequently resorts to outside counsel to lead the company's internal investigation of any material allegation of wrongdoing.

The advantages of using outside counsel are numerous. Most are quite obvious:

* Retained counsel can often bring a greater perception of objectivity to the task. Rather than being over-occupied by reporting lines, chains of command and internal protocols, outside counsel will often be sensitive to the needs of all of the client's corporate constituents (including shareholders) while keeping a keen focus on the "*end game*" – the need to later negotiate with prosecutors and regulators and to help the company mitigate its exposure.

* Outside counsel are often in a position to mobilize quicker, to bring greater resources to the task at hand and to undertake the assignment with vigor, freed from the day-to-day operational demands that can shackle in-house staff.

* Findings and recommendations, viewed often as coming from a fresh and unbiased review of the facts, can carry more authority internally with executive management and, certainly, at the Board level.

* Particularly if the engagement letter is crafted in a way to make clear that counsel's efforts are being undertaken in anticipation of litigation and so as to permit counsel better to advise management regarding legal matters (that is, that the work is covered by a legal privilege), the use of outside counsel provides the greatest assurance that management will retain maximum flexibility in terms of the ultimate disclosure of the results (and particulars) of the investigation to the government, shareholders, *etc.*

* Lower or mid-level employees having knowledge of critical facts may be more willing to divulge these facts to an outsider than to an internal investigator for fear, well-perceived or not, that the employee might be viewed by management, in later months or years, long after the investigation is concluded, as disloyal.

* Use of outside counsel can provide greater assurance to shareholders that the company is acting responsibly, and that the circumstances leading to the investigation will be unearthed, disclosed and fixed.
* Counsel may also be in a better position to provide expert legal advice as to potential violations of law, or as to potential financial liability exposure, especially if those matters pertain to an area requiring highly specialized legal assistance.

Most importantly, remember that prosecutors, agents and regulators are not infrequently skeptical of the results of purely internal efforts by a company to investigate its misconduct. While that skepticism is not going to go away simply because highly compensated outside counsel has been retained, prosecutors and agents know at some level that such counsel, as company outsiders having an independent interest in maintaining credibility with the government, may provide a stronger assurance of objectivity. All the better if the investigation is being led by an outside law firm employing one or more attorneys experienced in the investigation of complex financial and commercial criminal matters, knowledgeable as to the decision-making thought processes of prosecutors and regulators, and capable of communicating effectively with law enforcement authorities.

Beyond that, though, the quality of the company's investigation itself can be positively influenced by selecting specialists having significant experience in investigating matters in a grand jury setting and in preparing for criminal trials. While many lawyers who litigate commercial disputes can investigate, in the sense of being able to examine witnesses about documents and transactions, choosing a lawyer with deep *white-collar* investigations and prosecution experience can bring significantly added value. For example, counsel experienced in complex criminal investigations understand the importance of effectively planning for and "*sequencing*" witness interviews so that knowledge as to a particular topic is obtained incrementally, maximizing the accuracy and reliability of the information gleaned from the most important fact witnesses. This effort, often involving a good degree of subjective judgment and intuition, will entail arranging the order of interviews so as to build a foundation of knowledge derived from the early witness interviews to use when later speaking with the most important witnesses.

At other times, particularly in a fast-moving investigation or where witnesses might be anticipated to depart the company, counsel will not have that luxury and may need to expedite and "*lock in*" the account of a particularly important witness before the witness is lost or his or her recollection is tainted or inappropriately influenced. In those cases, a lot of early – and greatly expedited – work needs to be done in preparation, in terms of gathering documents and developing a working chronology from their review, so that the interviewer is able on the spot to effectively correct an errant or dissembling account by an uncooperative employee. Counsel specializing in investigating complex schemes are typically well experienced in preparing for the hard-to-interview witness.

Indeed, any counsel experienced in trial work, and particularly in criminal matters, will understand that an employee suddenly finding his or herself in the vortex of an investigation having criminal implications will as a witness be subject to a myriad of competing influences and motivations – fear, loyalty, friendship, self-preservation, not wanting to "*snitch*," and even the influence of the prospect of career advancement. Having spent years closely analyzing the weight of the evidence and the credibility of witnesses that will be offered both in support and in defense of criminal charges at a jury trial, seasoned white collar counsel can provide greater assurance that the facts developed during the investigation are accurate and can be relied on with confidence. In other words, appropriately experienced counsel can often better report to the company – and can more convincingly assure the government – that explanations of innocence by company employees, having been well-tested and challenged, are indeed accurate.

Notwithstanding outside counsel's role in improving the internal fact-finding process, the economic basis of the relationship between outside counsel and the company will also always tend to influence a perception by the government that the lawyer is "*being paid to say that*," when counsel is advocating – as is frequently the case – that the misconduct was committed by a relative small number of rogue employees, that the company has turned a new leaf, that it has implemented enhanced compliance protections, *etc.*

Exercising due diligence when selecting counsel is important. Management should ask: *What is the general reputation of the attorney within the legal community and among members of the judiciary? What exactly is his or her prior experience? Has it been predominately civil? Criminal? Has the attorney worked as a prosecutor? A regulator? Does counsel have a track record of aggressively squaring off with the government and other adversaries and taking matters to trial? Does counsel enjoy a good reputation with relevant prosecutors and regulators (and their offices and agencies)? Has he or she successfully assisted other companies navigate such waters in like settings, with like industries, or with respect to like allegations? What do other clients say about the work of the lawyer or the law firm?*

This sort of due diligence is often difficult to perform. It may be useful for management to involve one or more outside trusted advisors – business lawyers, accountants, sophisticated investors or board members – to help. Particularly where management is facing a "*bet the company*" encounter with the government, the company should avoid the temptation to hire one of its principal outside law firms simply out of convenience. While that firm may be perfectly suited to the task, the individual lawyer assigned to the matter is what counts. There may also be institutional factors that will appropriately give the company pause in selecting that firm to assist –- such as the fact that the law firm may have given advice to the company on an issue that is now part of the investigation, or that the length and financial significance of the relationship between the company and the firm might suggest to the government a lack of independence akin to the influences that might affect a lawyer on the "*in house*" corporate payroll.

Assuming the company has determined to select outside counsel to lead an investigation, what use of in-house counsel? In-house counsel are, of course, intimately familiar with the company, its culture and the personalities at play within the organization. They are known to management and employees and often seen as less of a threat. As a result, an important support role can be played by in-house counsel. In particular, counsel can be used to serve as a liaison, to lead efforts to gather documents, collect email traffic, conduct preliminary interviews, brief outside counsel, *etc.*, in a far less disruptive (and far less costly) manner than if these tasks were all assigned exclusively to outside counsel. Accordingly, in some limited circumstances, structuring of a hybrid approach – an investigation conducted at least in part by the in-house staff supervised by outside counsel – may be appropriate.

The Retention of the "Investigations Firm" or "Special Investigative Counsel."

There will be times where a matter to be investigated is of such sensitivity and magnitude that the Board will be influenced, for the sake of complete independence and the appearance of objectivity, to search for and retain a specialized *Investigations Firm*, never before used by the company, to do the bulk of the investigating. There exist today a number of such firms that operate regionally and nationally whose business is primarily to do forensic examinations and investigations. They are often staffed by counsel, but also by former federal and state law enforcement agents, forensic accountants, and IT experts. Many of these firms have central to their business model the assistance of companies caught up in complex, high stakes government investigations. Also, all of the Big 4 accounting firms have teams dedicated to helping clients having forensic and investigative support needs. Local or regional accounting firms can usually help too. Like hiring a law firm to do the work, using one of these options will be an expensive proposition. Still, because their involvement with the client are often *"one off"* forensic engagements, greater assurances may exist that the team will later be perceived as independent.

There are times, as well, when businesses may retain a law firm, on a one-time basis, as *Special Investigative Counsel* tasked with conducting – by itself or in collaboration with other investigative resources acting under counsel's direction – a top-to-bottom investigation under the ultimate supervision of the Board of Director's Audit Committee or a special Board committee responsible for the investigation. The use of *Special Investigative Counsel* might also be suggested by the involvement of the company's principal outside firm in the underlying matter or by the need to bring particularly specialized legal expertise to the task. One advantage of using a law firm as *Special Investigative Counsel* over the use of an *Investigations Firm* is the often-deeper legal bench strength brought by the law firm -- having, for example, the availability to call on different legal subject matter experts within the firm to help or the ability to enlist specialized resources to deal with collateral corporate governance issues. Obviously, the use of the *Investigations Firm* or *Special Investigatory Counsel* presents the greatest potential for disruption and cost to the company.

As has been suggested above, developing the right investigative approach will always appropriately be influenced by the legal landscape and the likelihood of enforcement consequences ahead, as well as by a host of pragmatic considerations. We suggest only that somewhere prominently in the decision-making mix must be counsel – for the sake of preserving the privilege; for helping to forecast and ultimately to influence the outcome of the matter that has captured (or may soon attract) the attention of government authorities; and for addressing the often-knotty legal issues that will invariably arise during the internal investigation.

The Role of Management and the Board During the Investigation

Management and a company's Board of Directors will have important responsibilities during any internal investigation, however staffed:

Supporting the Investigation.

For any internal investigation to succeed, it must have the support of management, genuinely committed to seeing the investigation to its conclusion, wherever it may lead. While decisions as to the scope and direction of the investigation, after initially arrived upon, are ordinarily left largely to those responsible for the investigation, management cannot divorce itself from the work ahead. The investigators need to be assured that management will review and bless any reasonable expansion of the investigation and will involve itself in the resolution of important strategic issues. During the *"active investigation"* stage, then, management ought neither be involved too much nor too little. Management should orient itself primarily to supporting the work of the investigators. There will be abundant direct management participation during the "*resolution and remediation*" stage.

Management should clearly designate a member of its team to serve as the management liaison to the investigators as well as to the Board during the investigation. Plainly, the company's selection of the person to so serve will send a message within the company as to how seriously committed the company is to the task and, as to any material allegation of wrong-doing, the company is well-advised to have a C-level member of the executive team (or internal General Counsel) serve in this leadership role. As to less serious allegations, that liaison might include a member of the in-house legal team, the Internal Auditor or the company's Compliance Officer. And, if the matter is itself being investigated by internal staff, management is particularly well advised overtly to manifest full support for the investigation and to message appropriately within the company the need for complete cooperation. It is important that persons of interest to the investigation understand that the matter at hand is not "*just another audit*" or part of some routine management review. Employees who may be required to provide testimony or other physical evidence need to understand the critical importance of honesty and integrity in dealing with even strictly internal investigative requests.

Protecting the Compliance "Process."

It is likewise important (and of great potential interest to the government) that, if the investigation was initiated as the result of an internal complaint, or due to the actions and external communications of a *whistleblower*, no personnel action is taken that might be perceived as retaliatory. Likewise, a promotion, favorable reassignment or the giving of a healthy bonus to a person reporting a matter might be perceived as designed to buy loyalty and silence or to shape later testimony. Accordingly, absent some exigency requiring a sanction, reassignment, *etc.*, management often should just let the pieces lie where they are and allow the investigation to run its course. If due to the passage of time some form of personnel action involving a whistleblower is required, labor and employment counsel should be consulted. Documentation of the basis for the action may prove critical.

Managing Internal and External Communications.

When facts prompting the need for an investigation become known, management will have an important role in managing the internal and external flow of information. The need to minimize rumors and to reduce the likelihood of a premature external disclosure of the existence of a controversy strongly counsels that, if the particulars of the matter are not generally known, information regarding the investigation be disseminated internally on a strict need-to-know basis. Counsel responsible for the investigation need the opportunity to quietly gather information and conduct preliminary interviews without undue distraction. Further, because securing physical evidence is of tantamount importance, counsel should be given full opportunity to do so before even internal disclosures are made within the business.

At some point, if for no reason other than to avoid speculation and rumor, management may deem it advisable to make a brief statement to employees more widely communicating the existence of an internal investigation and expressing management's commitment to a prompt and thorough review and resolution. For obvious reasons, that statement should be crafted and delivered only upon consultation with counsel. Similarly, a "*holding statement*" may need to be drafted for initial distribution to the media. No public statement regarding the results of an investigation should ever be disseminated until an investigation is complete.

Anticipating the Imposition of Sanctions -- Employee Discipline.

In the current regulatory environment, the government will expect a corporation promptly to discipline (if not discharge) employees complicit in misdeeds whether or not a regulatory action or prosecution is contemplated or eventually results. If it becomes apparent that an employee has engaged in criminal conduct, discharge is appropriate, even if the imposition of the sanction might prompt the employee to cooperate with the government in a larger investigation of the company or to go to the press. On the other hand, until the investigation is complete, or until actual misconduct is established, the company will be motivated and perhaps even required under its by-laws or otherwise, at law, to assist its employees and managers by securing for them independent counsel to aid in the defense of any external government investigation. Or if a suspension pending the conclusion of an investigation appears appropriate, the company may determine to do so *with pay* so as to demonstrate to other employees the company's belief that a termination should follow not just an investigation of wrongdoing but affirmative proof of actual misconduct. Tensions often result – the government does not look favorably upon corporate undertakings to keep on the payroll, or to advance legal fees for the benefit of, employees and managers who have in its estimation engaged in criminal misconduct. Again, counsel should be consulted regarding the resolution of all such questions.

What Say the Board and the Company's Outside Auditors?

Under the federal *Sarbannes-Oxley* legislation, publicly-traded companies have the affirmative obligation – through and under the supervision of its Board and its Audit Committee, or a special committee formed for that purpose – to investigate material allegations of financial wrongdoing and publicly to report significant irregularities. At times the Audit Committee may ask its auditors to assist or lead the effort to investigate allegations of financial errors or misfeasance, anticipating the possibility of the need for an earnings restatement. Beyond questions relating to the independence of the auditor, question may appropriately be raised later by the government as to whether the audit firm had the experience and forensic skillset necessary to such a task where there are potential criminal and other legal implications. Accordingly, where there are potential public financial reporting implications, outside counsel is often hired in lieu of the external auditor to investigate and report its findings directly to the Board or its Audit Committee. On other occasions not involving a publicly-traded company, where there is a suggestion of executive management complicity, or evidence that senior management condoned or failed appropriately to detect misconduct, the Board may be prompted directly to assume responsibility for the investigation in lieu of relying on management to lead the effort. Remember that board members have an affirmative fiduciary duty of care to the company, a duty that often requires their knowledge and oversight of the investigation of serious allegations of corporate improprieties.

Because the Board, as a practical matter, will not have the ability to facilitate the day-to-day gathering of evidence required in an investigation of any significance, there is likely to be some continued involvement of management in supporting the investigation even when the Board has essentially assumed its control. That is entirely appropriate. But it is very important, at the outset of the engagement, for the company to clearly identify for the company's lawyers who the client is. Who calls the shots? To whom will the results of the investigation be communicated? If the client is truly the Board of Directors, the engagement letter needs to say that. Reporting lines need to be drawn. Counsel needs to avoid internal conflicts and to understand clearly to whom it owes its duty of fidelity.

Invariably your outside public auditors are going to be keenly interested in the prompt investigation of any material allegation of financial wrongdoing. They themselves will want to investigate, or they will demand production of the work product of counsel retained to investigate the matter. Auditors may threaten withdrawal absent their demands being met. There will be a temptation, if for no reason other than to minimize cost and reducing disruptions, for management to ask counsel to share its work with the audit team.

These occasions raise difficult legal and practical issues. While an attorney's privileged and confidential work product can openly be discussed and shared within the client group, most assuredly an external audit firm for a client is not part of the lawyer's client group. Thus, disclosure by management to the external auditor of what the lawyer has said or concluded will likely be considered a waiver of the privilege. A lawyer's prudent refusal to share work product with the auditor, and his or her unequivocal advice to a client not to do the same, can lead to significant tensions.

The typical lawyer-accountant working solution – having the lawyer hire the accounting firm so as to permit the sharing of information under the umbrella created when accountants are hired explicitly to be the agents of the lawyer responsible for the forensic engagement – just does not work. Outside public auditors lose their independence when they become the agents of the company's lawyers subject to their direction, and only that degree of control and right to direct the auditors' work will serve to protect the lawyer's privilege. The solution also cannot be to have both teams of professionals investigate independently – the multiple and successive handling of witnesses and evidence by different teams of professionals is a recipe for disaster. Management will often need to huddle with its counsel and auditors to come up with a workaround. Sometimes attorney "*proffers*" of facts to the audit team may entirely satisfy the auditor. Those proffers typically involve narrative recitations, usually verbal, of the facts found to date by the investigating team (without disclosure of legal opinions or advice given to management, or of the precise contents of individual communications between attorney and client).

Other times no happy solution will be found. The audit team may be asked to defer its work. Or the lawyers may be asked to waive privilege. These are hard issues to resolve. The company needs to be thoroughly counseled regarding the legal risks inherent in each course.

Conducting the Investigation Itself

An "*investigation*" is simply the incremental process of gathering information and knowledge. It's a linear affair. Knowledge of the facts will be developed document-by-document, witness-by-witness until comfort in an ultimate finding is obtained. Counsel experienced in conducting investigations will know, however, that the process is not effectively discharged by simply gathering up evidence and witnesses and asking questions. Rather, any serious investigation involves a systematic study, proceeding largely in phases, starting with defining the scope and objectives of the matters to be investigated; securing and reviewing physical and electronic evidence; identifying through that review persons with pertinent knowledge; and, perhaps most important, sequencing interviews with sufficient precision so as to assure that credibility assessments can accurately be made and that the interviewer is armed with the results of the earlier interviews so as to prevent a purposefully evasive, crafty witness from effectively deflecting inquiries. Premature, wrongly-sequenced interviews can deprive the investigator of the ability to effectively challenge and confront the account of an errant employee intent on misleading the investigation. Ultimately, an interview conducted too early or without adequate preparation can not only create later credibility problems for the witness intent on misleading investigators but lead to a loss of investigative integrity in the eyes of the government or the Board sufficient enough to undermine the entirety of the effort.

Obtaining Physical Evidence and Documents.
The investigator must secure quickly all pertinent physical evidence and documents. The purposeful destruction of records or data by a manager, once uncovered by the government, is the quickest and surest way to insure his or her indictment. It could have disastrous results for the company as well. Counsel experienced in conducting investigations will have an inventory of items to be gathered (to include hard-copy documents, emails, notes, IMs and other electronic messages, calendars, telephone records, social media, *etc.*) and management should provide the support necessary to ensure that the task is accomplished and done so quickly. Counsel will appreciate the importance the government will later place on a company's not only appropriately preserving evidence, but of documenting the *"chain of custody"* and maintaining the integrity of evidence that might later be needed in court proceedings.

Because of the ubiquitous use by business organizations of central email and document servers, much of the initial document gathering and preservation can be done remotely and discretely by IT professionals. Use of enhanced *"predictive coding"* and other data search tools has in recent years made these early exercises much easier to accomplish. Yet, precautions need immediately to be taken to preserve evidence. The company's normal document retention (destruction) policy should be suspended. The regular practice of recycling data back-up tapes should likewise be abated. Individuals who might be viewed as "*subjects*" of the investigation ought not be asked to gather documents or electronic records. Rather, uninvolved personnel should be enlisted to assist. In more extreme cases, where spoliation of evidence is considered possible, internal audit or compliance staff may be enlisted to fan out and secure documents and IT professionals may be used to "*mirror image*" hard drives and secure laptops for review. That many employees use personal mobile devices and laptops to do company business can also present difficult employee privacy law issues when a company insists that, as a condition of employment, an employee must cooperate in allowing forensic access to the devices.

The disruption – and potentially adverse effects on morale – that might be occasioned by this process of gathering evidence from employees can be mitigated by a communication outlining the importance of document and data preservation in assuring the government and public of the integrity of the process. However, in so doing, management again needs to consult closely with counsel to ensure that any such internal communication not be misperceived or have unintended consequences. Company-wide communications relating to a matter under investigation need to be crafted with enormous care.

Arranging and Conducting the Employee Interview.

No amount of document review will substitute for interviews of persons with knowledge. In the context of a highly-charged interview of a manager or an employee potentially implicated in a scheme that has, or will likely, attract the attention of law enforcement, certain precautions should be undertaken and procedures followed.

Where the company's counsel is involved in the questioning, as will frequently be the case, it is critical that the employee-witness not misunderstand who the lawyer represents. The law requires that certain precautionary "*warnings*" be given to employees when interviewed by company-retained counsel to ensure that they understand that normal rules governing the confidentiality of communications between a client and his or her attorney do not apply to their session with the company's lawyers. These warnings include the admonition that:

*   Counsel (the interviewer) has been retained by management to conduct a thorough investigation of the matter at issue and that the company's principal interest is in determining the facts.
*   Counsel is meeting with the employee specifically in order to enable counsel to provide legal advice to the business.
*   Counsel – as a lawyer – represents the company and *not* the employee individually.
*   While the interview, as an internal corporate matter is confidential and legally privileged, it is the company and not the employee that owns and controls the privilege.
*   As a result, there may come a time when the company will determine to "waive" the privilege and divulge what is said during the interview to others, to include the government.

Somewhere in the giving of these "*Upjohn warnings*," counsel will typically inform the employee that the employee has a duty to cooperate and to provide truthful information. If the company has already determined that it will divulge the results of the interview to the government, the employee should be told that.

These so-called *Upjohn warnings* involve more than a little bit of mental gymnastics and can cause confusion and uncertainty in the employee that may get in the way of a free-flowing discussion of the facts. There should be no question remaining after their delivery that whatever is said during the interview will at a minimum be shared within the company, and perhaps to others, without the need to obtain permission from the witness. There should be no question remaining that the lawyer does not have an attorney-client relationship with the employee. The latter is challenging, however, as the employee knows that he or she is fact part – and sometimes a very important part – of the very company the lawyer represents (and what is a company, but for its people?) and that the lawyer will also implicitly or explicitly be asking the employee, on behalf of the company, to trust him or her and to tell all.

Counsel experienced in conducting employee interviews during internal investigations recognize the importance of fairly delivering these warnings and of later documenting their delivery. Counsel need to be adept at delivering these messages, and answering questions relating to them, in a clear and non-threatening way. There is, in fact, no need for the witness to perceive the instruction as a form of *warning* at all. Properly delivered, the discussion of these points can be viewed as informational and helpful to the witness who has most likely never before been involved in any internal controversy or scandal requiring a lawyer-led investigation.

There are other ground rules. If the employee has counsel with respect to the matter, the employee has the absolute right to have counsel present (assuming that the interviewer is counsel or is acting at the direction of counsel). However, the failure of an employee to agree to be interviewed (with or without counsel) may be grounds for discipline or termination – a fact that counsel may have to tell the employee if the employee proves uncooperative.

If the employee does not have counsel, there generally is no obligation to secure counsel for the employee. Indeed, many company-retained outside counsel hold the view that volunteering to supply the employee-witnesses a personal lawyer to attend an internal interview session is antithetic to a company's ability quickly and efficiently to obtain witness information. While the presence of counsel for the employee can in fact be very useful to the process of obtaining forthright accounts from witnesses, there is also the risk that counsel may insist that the interview be conducted only pursuant to a so-called "*joint defense agreement*," prompting a potential confrontation between employer and employee when later use of the information obtained is contemplated (a matter we discuss in Chapter III). Or the generosity of supplying counsel may be rewarded with delays occasioned by lawyer-scheduling challenges and, in the process, delay the completion of what has been planned as part of a precisely sequenced string of interviews.

Other interview and witness-handling best practices are either grounded in the law or have been learned through experience working with oft-internally-conflicted employees. The interviewer should be accompanied by a colleague principally responsible for taking notes. No other employees should be present. Group interviews are a non-starter. Verbatim notes should not be made. Such interviews should *never* be recorded. Never go "*off the record.*" Witnesses should be asked to keep the fact of the interview confidential. An internal, privileged work product memorandum of the interview should be prepared by counsel promptly after its conclusion. Distribution of the memorandum must be limited and should never be shared with the employee. Rarely should the witness be asked to sign a sworn statement of facts prepared by counsel or to otherwise commit his or her account in writing. Discussion should not be had with the witness or his counsel regarding what other employees have divulged. The company's "*position*" or even a characterization of the controversy should not be shared with the employee. Importantly, nothing should be said that might remotely be construed by the employee as dissuading the employee from talking to the government or doing anything other than telling the truth. It is sometimes advisable when dealing with the potentially difficult witness simply to inform the witness that all the interviewer is interested in is the truth and that no one, not the witness or the attorney, should be concerned about how the chips might eventually fall.

The Report of Investigation: When and To Whom Disclosed?

Neither the existence of nor particulars relating to the scope, progression and findings of any internal investigation should ever be disclosed outside of the company, except in the most selective and limited ways. Nothing could more delight class action or civil plaintiff's counsel than to be in possession of the negative conclusions of an independent investigator hired by a company. No one wants dirty laundry aired just as no one wants there even to be public discussion of sensitive internal matters relating to how well (or how poorly) employees or managers did their jobs. Internal investigations rarely result in the delivery to the company of an entirely clean bill of health or the exoneration of employees.

Accordingly, memoranda outlining the results and findings of a corporate internal investigation of allegations of material wrongdoing – and interim reports prepared along the way – should typically at the end of a matter be filed away and archived much like other highly sensitive and confidential corporate materials. In fact, they should rarely have achieved much circulation within the company even during the pendency of the inquiry. A strict need-to-know limit on dissemination is more than wise. And, absent extraordinary circumstances, such a report should never be shared with outsiders -- auditors, banks, investors or external public relations personnel, even pursuant to strict confidentiality understandings.

This especially holds true if the written reports at issue were prepared by counsel and are privileged. To preserve the privilege the company has an affirmative obligation to safeguard and prevent against inadvertent publication of the writings outside the company. Negligent handling of privileged materials can result in a finding that the company *waived* the attorney-client privilege with as much force and effect as if the business opted deliberately to waive and relinquish the privilege. Once the privilege is waived, the genie cannot be put back in the bottle. Any later claimant or person with a beef against the company can likely obtain the once-privileged material in court proceedings. Worse, if even one isolated privileged communication is deemed waived as to a particular subject of the lawyer's representation, a court might later find that there has been a broad *"subject matter waiver"* of the privilege. That is, the release of one privileged record might be held to require the production of any other privileged document on the same topic. Under this concept, the privilege as to the entirety of that *subject* is deemed waived.

This, then, leads to the question of what to give to the curious government prosecutor or regulator who has become aware (as seemingly always happens) that an internal investigation has been launched and has been concluded.

Some consideration at this point is appropriate of typical government expectations as to what happens to final or interim reports of internal investigations. The need for aggressive response to the financial scandals of the last 20 years has prompted the U.S. Department of Justice to articulate very clearly that one important factor it will take into account when exercising its considerable discretion as to whether it should proceed with criminal charges against a corporation is the degree to which the corporation has cooperated with the government. Indeed, in the not so distant past prosecutors were free to insist on waivers of the attorney-client privilege as a condition of leniency with respect to the filing of charges or as to the ultimate disposition of a matter. However, today, by Department of Justice policy promulgated in response to public and legislative criticism of these practices, a prosecutor may not demand such a waiver. However, consideration of the *extent* of the company's cooperation with the government – and the *completeness* of factual disclosures – remains an important and legitimate factor typically taken into account with respect to the prosecutor's charging decisions. Thus, while purely privileged material might not be directly demanded, there will often exist an expectation by investigating authorities -- stated or not -- that the lawyer-investigator will make an uninhibited disclosure of all that he or she knows.

Many other federal agencies and regulatory entities today require, or expressly reward, voluntary self-reporting (also without requiring an explicit waiver of the attorney-client privilege). The rewards to a company that qualifies as a first-reporter under the Department of Justice Antitrust Division's "amnesty" program can be immense, for example, often leading to a race by competitors to the doors of the Antitrust Division. The Securities and Exchange Commission requires disclosure of materially adverse facts (and also promises to reward only "*full cooperation*" when determining whether to initiate enforcement actions). Other agencies requiring or rewarding voluntary self-reporting include, among others, the New York Stock Exchange; agencies administrating federal government procurement programs; the Food and Drug Administration; OSHA; FINRA; the Environmental Protection Administration; and the HHS Office of Inspector General.

The expectations of these investigative or regulatory authorities will create pressure on the part of the business to disclose all manner of investigative work product in forms that, while perhaps falling short of the lawyer's ultimate and final expressions of factual and legal conclusions or the giving of legal advice, divulge at least indirectly the results of the lawyer's legal analysis and confidential communications conveyed to the attorney (*e.g.*, detailed and witness-specific proffers of fact; interview summaries; the identification of sources of information, *etc.*) The pressure to divulge all will be most heavily felt by a company that may be fearful of the devastating financial consequences of any adverse government action (such as a federal debarment, massive fines or even an indictment, all of which play very poorly in the capital markets).

Here are two immediate problems relating to any contemplated government disclosure – and a possible solution.

First, a disclosure to the government of privileged information is a disclosure to the world. Some companies have argued that there is sound policy to support a finding that a disclosure of privileged material to the government should be deemed a "*limited waiver*," applicable only to the specific government agency at issue. While that argument has achieved some traction with a few courts, most courts do not recognize the concept. A waiver is a waiver.

Second, attempts to achieve only a selective or "*partial waiver*" (*i.e.*, the argument that a waiver of limited privileged materials, an interview report, for example, should be deemed to be a waiver only as to that specific document or communication) are not favored. As noted, many courts embrace the notion of there being a subject matter waiver flowing from *any* deliberate waiver of the privilege as to a particular subject. In other words, production to the government of a few isolated interview reports penned by a company's lawyer may result in a finding that the privilege has been waived in all respects as to the entirety of the subject of the matter being investigated. The danger here is not so much that the *government* might get the additional records that had withheld from production (as the government will typically honor an agreement to receive tailored company disclosures without considering it to be an expansive waiver of the privilege applicable to all communications on the subject). Rather, a finding of the occurrence of a broad subject matter waiver will open the door to any and all third parties not party to the intended government-only disclosure to argue that the waiver permits access by all outside parties.

So, what to tell the government at the end of the investigation? The company can reasonably assume that some disclosure of the results of the investigation is going to be required by the government, particularly if the prosecutor or regulator has agreed to defer or limit its own investigation until the company has finished its work.   Does that mean the company's relinquishment to the government of a final report of investigation in the very form that has been delivered to management and the Board, containing no-holds-barred assessments of complicity and fault and detailed recommendations regarding the need for remediation? Or, should it entail a more selective production of materials, such as interview memoranda of most likely interest to the government?

Fortunately, there are ways for a company to make disclosures that will satisfy most prosecutors and regulators without incurring a finding that there has been a waiver of privilege. The attorney-client privilege protects confidential *communications* between lawyer and client and not the *information* a lawyer might learn from his or her client, the company. It is usually perfectly appropriate for counsel to make a verbal recitation (or a written summary) of *information and facts* to the government without revealing directly or by implication a single confidential communication that took place between a specific employee and the lawyer. There is actually a difference in terms of the preservation of the attorney-client privilege between, on the one hand, the lawyer reporting to the government, "*The light was green,*" and, on the other hand, the lawyer reporting, "*John told me the light was green.*" The disclosure of only the latter is a deliberate waiver of the privilege. And yet, through the former disclosure, the government has been given the information it needs (and the ability to direct the powerful tools it has towards gathering for itself the evidence it may or may not need), while the lawyer has protected his or her confidential conversations with the client's employees.

These sorts of abbreviated disclosures can be made in different ways. They might take the form of a somewhat sanitized version of the final report of investigation, delivered to the government as a confidential settlement communication devoid of explicit reference to witness accounts and legal conclusions. They might take the form of a demonstrative-aid and documented-assisted presentation of facts. They might be purely verbal. These sorts of informal *proffers*, such as those discussed earlier in this Chapter with respect to external auditors, are made not infrequently to the seeming satisfaction of prosecutors and regulators who respect that companies need to be able to be free, in a privileged and confidential way, and without fear of a finding of waiver, to engage in self-policing, self-reporting and publicly-beneficial self-assessments of its conduct.

Beyond the fact that prosecutors are no longer by policy to insist that companies waive the attorney-client privilege as a condition for getting co-operation credit, the amount, detail and form of the disclosure that will satisfy a particular prosecuting office is all going to depend on the severity and pervasiveness of the misconduct. No hard and fast rules apply. Whether the disclosure is to be made through a verbal presentation or written report, and corresponding issues relating to the form or detail of either, are matters that need to be worked out to the satisfaction of the government -- and, of course, of the company -- case-by-case.

Chapter 2

The Unanticipated Search Warrant

Federal and state law enforcement agents have many tools at their disposal when conducting investigations. Some of their more commonly used investigative techniques are relatively non-intrusive and particularly well-suited for the investigation of business crimes and regulatory infractions: informal witness interviews; grand jury subpoenas to compel the production of documents and the appearance of witnesses; court orders mandating the production of IT, social media, messaging and telephone data; judicial *letters rogatory* for foreign sources of evidence; agency-to-agency sharing requests; and, of course, the reliance on the accounts of cooperating witnesses and whistleblowers. There are, however, in addition, many more exotic and invasive means of gathering real-time evidence – these include telephone wiretaps, room bugs, undercover informants, consensually-monitored telephone calls, the use of "*body wires,*" as well as live electronic and physical surveillance. Which of these various investigative tools law enforcement will use depends tremendously upon the nature of the offenses being investigated and the stage of the investigation.

Clients, alarmed and worried after learning that the government may be investigating them, not infrequently ask, "*Are our phones being tapped?,*" "*Do you think he will be 'wearing a wire'?,*" "*Are our computers being monitored?*" The answer to all of these sorts of questions is usually, "*No.*" It is very difficult for the government to establish, in an investigation focusing largely on historic commercial transactions and events, the legal requirements the courts insist must be met before authorizing the use of eavesdropping activities, such as the installation of a wiretap. These surveillance tools are also enormously resource intensive in terms of the effort required by the agents, prosecutors and the courts to obtain, approve and maintain their use. But, as importantly, the government does not often consider these types of investigative strategies to be very effective in the business crimes context, and particularly not after an investigation has become "*overt*," or public, and subject to being known to the person or business being investigated. Law enforcement agents understand the risk that, unless an investigation is deeply "*covert*," the target or subject of an investigation who imagines he or she is under investigation will attempt to "*cleanse*" themselves by offering false explanations to colleagues, associates or former "*co-conspirators*." There is not much more powerful defense evidence than a target's recorded explanations of innocence given to a third party at a time when there was no particular reason to believe that he or she was being recorded.

In this Chapter, we address one particularly intrusive and disruptive technique being used in business investigations that was once largely reserved for use in the investigation of more tawdry offenses, such as narcotics trafficking, child porn, racketeering and violent crimes: the *search warrant*.

Execution of a court-ordered search warrant has become a relatively common strategy employed by the government in the investigation of businesses. The unanticipated appearance of officers clad in full law enforcement regalia to seize business records and computers is increasingly used today not only here in the United States but by regulatory authorities in Europe and Asia (where they are called "*dawn raids*") in the investigation of truly "*paper*" offenses, to include complex antitrust, trade and intellectual property investigations. Gone are the days where the government feels itself constrained to rely on the good will of a corporation to produce to the government, through the paper subpoena process, all responsive documents and other tangible evidence requested of the business.

Yet, in more routine cases, and particularly in those cases where there is no particular reason to suspect that efforts will be made to obstruct the government's investigation, the effort involved in mobilizing for a search warrant requires considerable justification for its use. And, as is the case of the use of forms of electronic surveillance, agents and the prosecutors working with them will not ordinarily use a search warrant where they believe that the individual or company under investigation is aware that there is an on-going investigation. In that context, where the investigation is overt, chances are substantially increased that the documents, files and computer records to be seized have already been marshaled and are in the possession of counsel. Thus, when making an application to the court for the issuance of a search warrant, the agents and prosecutors will ordinarily be facing circumstances wherein the government believes that it needs to rely on the element of surprise to obtain quickly all available records without interference in the evidence-gathering process by the errant employee or manager – or by meddlesome counsel. Because that element of surprise is critical to the value and success of the use of a search warrant, the execution of a warrant is sometimes the first indication to a business that the government is conducting a criminal investigation. Management will typically have had little if any forewarning that the government is interested in the company, much less that it was contemplating the use of a warrant.

A Hypothetical -- Managing the Search Warrant "*Fire Drill*"

Consider the following hypothetical scenario that might face a member of a management team, or counsel, responsible for handling the company's response to a government search:

At the beginning of the business day, while you are on travel, you receive a call from your Controller at the Genetics Division headquarters on the west coast. She advises that she is also out of the office but had just gotten off the telephone with their receptionist, who reported that approximately 20 "agents" wearing guns and raid jackets had arrived 15-20 minutes ago, announced that they were executing a search warrant and entered the premises. According to the receptionist, the authorities were wearing jackets identifying themselves as from the FBI and OIG, although there were also a handful of local policemen in full uniform. Your Controller tells you that although the receptionist is really frightened, the authorities were behaving professionally.

Your several subsequent calls to the Genetics Division COO and CFO to find out what was occurring on the scene go unanswered. No one is picking up the telephone at all. Within 20 minutes you receive another call, this time from your Division Assistant Controller on his cellphone. Practically whispering, he reports that employees have all been gathered together in an assembly room and are being taken out one by one to be questioned by the agents. Also, he reports that a few minutes ago the agents, with the assistance of your Division IT manager, began identifying and boxing up physical files and a few laptops. One agent has already walked away with what appeared to be the CFO's desktop server. He reports that all the employees have been told that they cannot make telephone calls (apparently why he was whispering) or leave the premises until the agents "processed them."

Within an hour of the arrival of the agents, while you are on the telephone talking to your in-house attorneys, you get a report that a television crew has arrived at the Division offices and is filming the coming and going of agents and employees from across the street.

A business can never truly plan for the execution of a search warrant. It presents the worst sort of "*fire drill*" – and, like a fire or natural disaster, the crisis will develop without warning. An overbroad seizure of business records and computers can cause massive disruption to any business. By virtue of the press coverage alone – including the prospect of video footage soon to be seen by customers, investors and suppliers of raid-jacketed agents carrying boxes of records and computers from the premises – the execution of a search warrant at a legitimate place of business can be disastrous. Managers and employees, taken entirely by surprise, may well be interviewed by law enforcement on substantive topics without any knowledge of the reasons for the raid and without an effective ability to consult with counsel. Highly confidential and proprietary information may be seized, and legally privileged attorney-client correspondence, emails and memoranda may end up in the hands of the government. Unfortunately, there may be little if anything a company can do to slow the process down. There will be no ability whatever to suspend or stop it entirely.

Although far from an everyday occurrence, the use of a search warrant to investigate business crimes happens frequently enough, particularly in regulated industries, that it is prudent for most businesses to spend some time contemplating how a company ought to respond, no matter how remote seems the prospect of its occurrence. Execution of a search warrant of a business usually takes many hours and implicates numerous legal and practical issues requiring immediate and deft attention and resolution. While de-escalation, maintaining order and minimizing business disruption will be the first priority for the manager on the scene, we will address a number of best practices that should be followed to protect the interests of the company.

Ultimately, as the discussion below will demonstrate, the contingency merits the development of basic internal protocols and the training of select staff as to what to do during the intense early moments of the execution of a warrant. It might sound strange for any legitimate business to undertake to train personnel as to the occurrence of a law enforcement raid. But, because the execution of a search warrant is no longer reserved for use in the investigation of criminal enterprises, preparation for it by a business of any complexity and size is only prudent. Just as a business should expect there to be no raised eyebrows amongst employees asked to participate in training in anticipation of a spot inspection by a regulator, or in connection with the company's procedures relating to the acceptance of a court-issued subpoena or of other official pleadings served by a process server, such training when appropriately and discretely presented to the limited company personnel who will most likely directly interface with the government during the execution of a search warrant – receptionists, facility operations management and IT personnel – need not cause alarm or rumor that the company is preparing to be *"raided by the police."*

A company imagining itself at risk of the arrival of agents someday to execute a search warrant might pose a number of questions to its lawyers:

Under what legal authority can the government search a business? If raided, can a business go to court and ask it, on an emergency basis, to suspend the search so that the company can properly understand the authority of the agents to proceed?

Can a company petition a court – or simply demand of the agents – that the scope of the search be limited?

What about confidential and proprietary business data, as well as privileged attorney-client communications? Can the business prevent the agents from taking those?

Can the business prevent or limit the dismantling and seizure of servers and work stations necessary to its operations?

Can company lawyers enter the offices to observe the search?

How long can agents keep records and computers before having to give them back?

How can a company stop agents from using their presence at the business in connection with the execution of the search warrant as a means to interview employees? Do employees have the right to have lawyers present to help them with the interviews?

Should employees ever be instructed not to cooperate or provide information?

What should be said to the media? Should a press release be issued so that investors will not become alarmed?

What should a company say to its employees during and after the search?

The Source and Scope of the Government's Authority to Execute a Search Warrant

Unlike compliance with a subpoena, which involves the orderly gathering by its addressee of responsive records and later production at a pre-scheduled time and place, a search warrant issued under federal or state judicial authority enables (in fact, commands) the executing law enforcement agents to enter a business, even forcibly, and to seize items identified in the warrant. The warrant is a court-issued writ. It is a judicial demand that the government execute the warrant according to its terms, and an employee that gets in the way of its execution will have consequences to pay.

Our constitution requires that a search warrant be issued by a neutral judicial officer only after the court has made a specific finding that *"probable cause"* exists to believe that evidence of specifically-identified criminal activity is actually then located at the business. The courts do not on their own decide whether a search warrant should be used and they are never involved in determining the relative timing of the execution of a warrant during a government investigation. Rather, the judge (or more commonly a magistrate) issues the warrant on the strength of a detailed affidavit submitted by the investigating *"case agent"* specifying the evidentiary basis for the government's belief that precisely identified crimes were committed and further demonstrating with particularity the likelihood that documents and other things evidencing the crime are in fact still located at the places to be searched. Thus, while search warrants are issued by the courts, they will not issue without prompting and direction from the government.

By law, agents executing a warrant must be precisely guided as to what they can seize. The issuance of a warrant will never enable the government to conduct a fishing expedition into the files of a business. The items to be seized must be stated on the face of the warrant itself, and described with particularity. A search warrant is defective if, due to its vagueness, it authorizes the agents to make a generalized, unfocused search of the premises. Documents and other evidence seized outside the identified scope of the warrant, or pursuant to a warrant that is insufficiently particular or inadequately supported by evidence amounting to probable cause, may be ordered returned to the business or may be deemed inadmissible for use during court proceedings. Assuming, however, that the warrant is proper, the agents armed with a warrant can look unsupervised throughout the business for the things authorized to be seized. If in the course of that search they inadvertently find in open view other evidence not specifically identified in the warrant, they are usually entitled to take that too.

In the business crimes context, and particularly in federal cases, it is safe to assume that an investigation has been underway for days or weeks or even months before the warrant was obtained, and that a prosecutor has been working closely with the agents to determine the necessity for and scope of the search. As suggested above, a search warrant typically is sought in a business crimes context where prosecutors believe that there exists the possibility that the service of a subpoena may prompt an employee to hide or destroy records, or in other circumstances where there exists some unique exigency. A search warrant is not only intrusive and disruptive to a business. Its planning and execution involves a lot of work, analysis, manpower and advance planning on the government's part. The agents on the scene, armed with full judicial authority to enter the premises and to seize the evidence specified, have no obligation – and typically have no inclination – to negotiate regarding the scope and manner of the search.

A warrant may only be executed at the precise business location specified on the face of the warrant and then only during daylight hours. A warrant issued commanding the search of a particular facility does not enable the agents to enter into an adjoining or nearby (but separate) building or complex, no matter how closely connected that facility is to the premises identified in the warrant and no matter whether the search of the premises named in the warrant leads the agent to conclude that the evidence to be seized is actually in the separate facility. In such a case, an entirely new warrant must be obtained (although the agents are allowed to surveil the separate premises and limit access to and from the site while the new warrant is being obtained).

It is important to recognize here that law enforcement officers may also obtain access to a business and search it through another less forceful means – the *"consent search."* The law liberally recognizes the government's right to search a business or residence if an appropriately-authorized person consents to the search without the necessity of the government having to procure a warrant and without even the agents having to have probable cause to ask to conduct the search. Generally speaking, it is best that a business not consent to an open search of its premises or files, no matter how narrow the request. While a business will want to serve as a good corporate citizen and to cooperate with reasonable government inquiries, circumstances suggesting that law enforcement agents or regulators are seeking evidence of misconduct portends the possibility of outcomes that can involve criminal charges and literally years of litigation and bad collateral consequences ahead. A search warrant appropriately guides the discretion of agents on the scene as to what may be taken away and permits a later challenge to a misguided government search. Accordingly, it should be the exceedingly rare occasion where a company consents to an unannounced warrantless search of its premises.

We discuss *consent searches* here because management must be mindful that agents may, during the execution of a search warrant, ask for consent to search for documents and things not identified in the warrant or to search premises beyond those specified. A request to expand the search may need not explicitly use the term *"consent"* and can be as informal as, *"We're going to look over here too, is that Ok?"* or, *"We're going to take this too, do you mind?"* Any indication of assent to the request will likely be treated as the giving of legal consent to the expansion of the warrant's terms. The manager on the scene, having pledged the company's cooperation and being not particularly focused on the precise scope of the warrant-specified *"items to be seized,"* is going to feel compelled to agree to the request made by the reasonable-appearing agent on the scene. Rarely, however, should such consent be given. The government will have in these circumstances decided to proceed formally, without warning, with a disruptive, invasive and involuntary search authorized by a court. It is usually far better for all that all parties play by the well understood rules and limitations prescribed by law relating to the obtaining and execution of search warrants. Providing on-the-fly informal verbal consent to agents to exceed the scope of their warrant authority will almost always be problematic if questions later arise regarding the propriety and scope of the expanded search. A polite response, to the effect of, *"You're of course free to take anything the warrant permits you to take,"* should suffice.

When Agents Arrive

Needless to say, the execution of a search warrant at a business is an extraordinary event – the element of surprise will not infrequently provoke a level of stress and uncertainty conducive to the making, on the part of the surprised manager on the scene, error and misstep. Thus, despite the infrequency of the event, a business will always benefit by having an established protocol for dealing with a search warrant. Because a receptionist will typically be the first point of contact with law enforcement, he or she should know who in management to call and to know the identity of the manager's back up. The manager responsible for liaising with the government will likewise need to know which attorney to call and what facts that lawyer will need to know. Presumably a company's in-house counsel is not going to have much experience with search warrants and the most effective call for help will be to counsel with some experience with law enforcement. Not infrequently, if not planned and pre-determined, that call will probably be to a lawyer the company has not dealt much with before (it's a *criminal defense lawyer*, after all) and the conversation is going to have to be rushed. The manager on the scene will also need to understand how appropriately to interface with the law enforcement agents on the scene.

We identify below search warrant response best practices. We start, however, by approaching the scene from the perspective of the law enforcement agents responsible for the lawful, effective and safe execution of the warrant.

The Commencement of the Search – the Law Enforcement Search Team

Assuming the warrant was issued by a federal court, any federal agent having criminal law enforcement authority can assist in the execution of a warrant. Agents of the Federal Bureau of Investigation, Department of Homeland Security (including Immigration and Customs Enforcement), Secret Service, IRS, Drug Enforcement Administration, Fish and Wildlife Service, and Food and Drug Administration, among many other federal agencies, may, in connection with one of their criminal investigations, seek the issuance of a search warrant. Other agencies, such as the Securities and Exchange Commission, having no independent criminal enforcement jurisdiction, need to enlist the help of a law enforcement agency with independent authority to prosecute relevant financial crimes (such as the FBI) to forcibly seize records from a business. Sometimes, however, these latter agencies not possessing specific *criminal* enforcement authority can obtain the emergency appointment of a receiver who will be empowered by the court to enter a business and seize its records with like effect. Rarely would a receiver take such a step without support from federal law enforcement agents acting in much the same manner as they would when executing a search warrant. State authorities, for their part, also have broad independent authority to obtain search warrants, and state and local law enforcement commonly accompany federal agents during the execution of federal warrants.

Because of the logistics involved in successfully -- and safely -- executing a search, the lead agency in the investigation will typically gather together a team of agents shortly before its execution, brief the team generally as to the nature of the case and any security concerns, "*stage*" the search, make individual assignments of responsibility and arrange for the team to travel together to the premises. Most of the agents at the scene will know very little about the investigation or about the business itself. It is not unusual to have 20 or more agents assigned to the search of a business, but a search warrant can be executed by as few as two to three officers. The agents usually wear blue raid jackets identifying their agency. Due to manpower limitations, or because an investigation is being conducted jointly by two or more agencies, or by a "*task force*," the agents on the scene will often represent multiple agencies. At times, as noted, local law enforcement officers are enlisted to help. There will, however, always be a lead agent on the scene assigned to supervise the search. That agent is usually the "*case agent*," having the most knowledge of the investigation. At other times the lead agent on the scene will be the case agent's "*group supervisor*." The prosecutor involved in the preparation and presentation of the search warrant application to the court may or may not have been much involved in the investigation but will typically, at a minimum, be on call to handle any questions the agents have while at the scene. More often than not though, particularly in a business crimes context, the prosecutor will have been intimately involved in the investigation leading to the search. In either scenario, however, it is unusual for the prosecutor to be on the scene accompanying the search team.

Because it is an intrusive law enforcement encounter with persons unexpected to deal with it, the agents asked to help execute the warrant will have been briefed and mindful of physical security concerns. The agents will also be sensitive to the possibility of the destruction of evidence. The agents will be motivated, then, particularly in a case where the items to be seized are extensive, to obtain firm control over the site as quickly as possible. Accordingly, there may be very limited opportunity to start a dialogue with the lead agent before the agents have fanned through the premises, identified themselves to employees and asked the employees to gather their personal possessions and assemble in a location away from their work stations or offices.

These events can intimidate and scare employees. Agents are usually very professional. They do not draw weapons. But they are trained to move quickly and assertively to gain physical control and to assure themselves that no threat to their person exists. The opening moments of the execution of a warrant are usually adrenaline charged. There is typically no dawdling and little opportunity for negotiation or even discussion. Yet, as we describe below, the dust will soon begin to settle and there will be time for the business to approach the events in an orderly way, watchful for the preservation of the company's rights and interests.

Management's Initial Encounter with Law Enforcement

The senior-most manager responsible for the physical plant being searched is well-advised to approach the opening phase of the search of the business as follows:

* Together with another manager or employee who can serve as a witness, **locate the lead or "case" agent**. Ask to see a copy of the warrant. Ask, if appropriate, to see a copy of the agent's credentials (this may better identify the agent's employing agency). While the agent must present for inspection a copy of the search warrant, the government need not delay the commencement of the search while dealing with such preliminaries. It is not unusual for the search to be underway before or while this initial encounter is occurring.

* ***Read the warrant and the accompanying description of the items to be seized*** (all told the document will typically be two to five pages in length depending upon the degree of specification of the things to be seized). The agent has no obligation to produce a copy to be kept by the business, although the agent will likely honor a request that the company be allowed to photocopy it. The business is not entitled to inspect the search warrant *application* or the underlying affidavits prepared by the agents submitted to the court in support of the application. Because details of the investigation contained in the application materials may reveal the identity of confidential sources of information, applications are maintained by the courts "*under seal*" and are confidential.

* Although the agent will have no obligation to do so, ***ask the agent what the warrant is about.*** Whatever he or she says, do not comment, argue or attempt to engage in a dialogue about the wisdom of the investigation. The agents are not going to leave.

* ***Assure the agent that the company will cooperate.*** Offer to provide a conference room or some other area to serve as the agents' on-site headquarters. An offer of coffee, space, telephone assistance and other amenities will often be accepted and, either way, the offer will set a constructive tone that may be helpful later in the day.

* ***Offer IT assistance.*** The government will typically arrive with one or more agents or technicians having expertise in conducting computer searches. To minimize the impact of any proposed seizures of computer equipment or data (as well as to serve as witness to the seizures that occur), it is always prudent to immediately offer to the government IT assistance and to summons the company's IT manager to help.

* ***Project an attitude of calm and reasonableness.*** Cooperation is the order of the moment. The agents are executing a search warrant because they believe that documents might be destroyed or because there exists some other exigency. They will not know much about the business, its employees or culture. Defusing initial hostility or

suspiciousness with an early commitment of cooperation will go a long way toward the success of later efforts during the warrant's execution to negotiate reasonable limits as to what the agents are seizing or the manner in which the search is being conducted.

* During this initial encounter with the agent, *make a complete mental note of information that will need to be reported to company counsel* -- the agencies involved, the nature and scope of the documents to be seized, and the number of agents on site.

* At some point very early on, *advise the agent that it is necessary to call and report to counsel.* The agent does not have the authority to prevent the company from doing so, but he or she may attempt to discourage it. The agent should be assured that the business needs to confer with counsel to ensure that the company is reacting to the warrant appropriately and persist, calmly.

* No matter the temptation, it is advisable that *no effort should be made – at least during this very initial stage – to negotiate a limitation of the search.* The agents need to get over the initial rush before processing company objections or requests for scope limitations, no matter how reasonable the requests. There will usually be plenty of time once matters have calmed to address scope issues. Efforts in these early moments should be directed towards defusing a potentially hostile encounter and towards making as many factual observations as can be made to report to counsel.

What to do if the facility searched is staffed minimally or is overseen by less senior (and untrained) members of the management team having limited authority to speak for the company? A more senior manager not at the scene should be assigned to take charge and to contact the manager at the facility to help externally. A designated representative of the company not at the scene at the commencement of the search may attempt to go to the facility and enter, but he or she will be likely met at the entrance by an agent who appropriately can for security purposes deny access to the public, employees and outside personnel and management. If met with such opposition, the company's representative seeking entry should simply explain the company's interest in making sure that any concerns during the search are appropriately addressed. The representative should ask, if necessary, to speak to the case agent and, if these efforts fail, call counsel to enlist his or her assistance in getting an appropriate company representative access to the premises.

Obtaining the Assistance of Counsel

Counsel having experience with search warrant execution issues can provide invaluable assistance to the company during the search. Typically, trusted outside corporate or litigation counsel for any business will have little or no experience in dealing with search warrant issues and, unless the company has already specifically retained counsel with criminal defense capacity, the company's outside attorney will immediately set out to contact a colleague with experience in criminal investigations to assist. That practitioner, in turn, will need very quickly to communicate with the company and to mobilize readily available legal resources as necessary. In these situations, counsel may make plans to travel to the location of the search. Just as with occasions when a senior manager seeks access to a facility being searched, the lead agent may or may not allow counsel into the premises. But, no matter the degree of the attorney's access to the facility or to agents conducting the search, there will be plenty to do at the scene. The presence of a legal team permits immediate access by management to counsel positioned to communicate face-to-face with the agents and is important to the company's ability to debrief employees and supervisors as they leave the premises. Ideally, outside counsel should be contacted, then, as soon as possible after the company's first communication with the agents.

If, as often happens, the company's principal outside attorney is not immediately available to be on site, colleagues might be sent with specific tasks to be accomplished at the scene. The lead attorney asked to help will, whether at the scene or not, be in frequent telephonic contact with senior management and other members of the legal team dispatched to help.

In addition to providing real-time guidance and advice to management, counsel with experience in addressing business-related search issues can greatly assist the business in dealing with the warrant and its aftermath, by among other things:

* Communicating directly with the agents regarding the scope of the search and logistical issues that threaten an undue disruption of the business.

* Communicating and negotiating directly with the prosecutors or lead case agent when material legal issues arise (*e.g.,* overbroad seizures of computers, records and things, the review of legally privileged materials, inappropriate behavior or substantive interviewing of employees and managers).

* Seeking in appropriate (and extreme) cases emergency Magistrate-Judge review of the manner in which the warrant is being executed.

* Debriefing employees as they leave the business – this is a very important fact-gathering task (and why counsel usually go to the scene) as it sheds immediate light on the scope and seriousness of the investigation and it may provide information critical to a subsequent motion for return of property, to suppress the fruits of the search, or to obtain the return or protection of attorney-client communications and proprietary information.

* Advising management regarding the company's communications with employees during the search and in the days following.

* Helping assess the scope of the search, and to determine whether the agents have exceeded that scope by seizing items not authorized to be seized or by searching premises not authorized to be searched.

* Advising the business as to appropriate responses to media inquiries.

Dealing with Employee Interviews at the Scene

Agents have no authority to detain employees for any significant period of time after the initiation of a search. Nonetheless, and particularly at the beginning stages of the search, if employees ask if they are free to go, the agents may well tell the employees that they must stand down and wait. Indeed, in the interest of conducting a *"security sweep"* and to otherwise secure the premises, the agents tasked with executing the warrant will often be asked to *"process"* the employees located in the critical areas being searched before they are allowed to leave the business. The resulting agent-employee interactions can be as benign as the agent's asking for the employee's name, contact information, position, work station or location, *etc.* At other times, however, agents have been known to use the situation – to include the element of surprise and the unpreparedness of employees and managers – to ask more *"substantive"* questions relating to their investigation. In fact, the agents may seek actually to interview mid-level or senior management level employees about the matter, even in circumstances where the agents have reason to believe, or may actually know, that the company has retained counsel relating to the controversy.

Practically speaking, there is very little that can be done to stop or limit such interviews. Outside counsel should be informed if employees are being held for any extended period of time. Counsel should also immediately be told if the agents are attempting to interview mid-level or senior management employees who would have had the authority to act, speak for or *"bind"* the company as to any of the issues or transactions that appeared to have led to the investigation. If the company is not, under these latter circumstances, able to obtain the immediate intervention of counsel, its representative on the scene should inform the case agent of the fact that the company has engaged counsel as to the matters covered by the warrant and that such questioning is more appropriately to occur in the presence of counsel. While company counsel may not be deemed to represent individual lower-level employees without their explicit assent to the representation, the same may not necessarily be said for more senior level employees who might be considered to have authority to act or speak for the client-company itself.

In these circumstances, interviews of managers will probably stop. However, the agents on the scene may persist. Under no circumstances should the company's representative become even remotely belligerent or aggressively seek to terminate the interviews. This may only later be viewed as an effort to obstruct the investigation or the search. If anyone, counsel should take the lead when attempting to terminate substantive interviews.

As alluded to above, counsel's de-briefing, whether at the scene or not, of employees who were very recently questioned by the agents can be indispensable to an understanding of the scope of the investigation and of the agents' views as to the involvement of the company (or individual managers) in suspected misconduct. This debrief can also be used to apprise employees that, while they are free to communicate to agents about the company's business should there be follow up inquiries, they are free also not to communicate with the agents. The manner in which this is articulated is very important lest employees later claim that they were discouraged from communicating or cooperating with the law enforcement agency involved. The employees can also be told at that time that the company itself has counsel and that legal representation of the employee will be provided (if the company sees that as appropriate) in connection with any future law enforcement inquiries should the employee request legal help.

This initial debrief of employees must be done by counsel. It is fair game for the company's attorneys to ask employees about the action of the agents in conducting the search and about the questions the agents are asking. The employees will be upset and potentially later confused, however, as to what was asked of them at the scene by the agents and then later by the company's attorneys. Counsel for the business, armed with a clear agenda as to what ought to be asked of the employees and of the advice that should be given to them, are in a far better position to fend off later claims of harassment of employees or of obstructive behavior than will be members of the management team.

Counseling Employees

Needless to say, employees will want to obtain assurances from their bosses regarding the meaning and implications of the fact that their place of employment has just been raided. Management should resist the temptation to discuss the situation with individual employees or with groups of employees at the time of the search. The company may assure the employees equally well simply by having leadership display an air of confidence and by advising employees that the company has pledged its cooperation. The company may well also indicate, if appropriate, that there will be a meeting or communication in the next few days to address the search.

Remember that, following as stressful an encounter as the intrusion by law enforcement officers into their place of work, employees will likely not accurately remember what individual managers have told them or may misconstrue their words. For management's part, no one will likely have a prepared script and there is risk of imprecise communication and misstatement. Accordingly, as difficult as it may be, senior management should resist the urge to talk substantively or to declare the company's innocence. Rather, management should let the situation defuse and address the employees only after having had time for reflection. Counsel should be in a position to advise the company precisely as to what should be said to employees after the search. Ideally, days will have passed and management will have prepared comments or talking points in hand when addressing employees.

Protecting the Attorney-Client Privilege

Should the agents appear to be seizing computers indiscriminately, servers and hard-copy files, questions will arise as to the agents' sensitivity towards the privileged nature of legally-confidential files containing attorney-to-client and client-to-attorney communications. Generally speaking, and as discussed earlier in Chapter I, a document is privileged and absolutely protected from disclosure (and seizure) if it constitutes or reflects any communication between the company and its lawyers that is intended to have been confidential and that was for the purpose, directly or indirectly, of obtaining or giving legal advice or assistance. The legal privilege is quite broad. Even very routine communications, such as records showing the transmittal of documents to the company's lawyers, and thus showing the scope of topics the lawyer has been asked to assist with, may fall within the scope of one or more forms of legal privilege. While the privilege exists to support important public policy interests, its protections are easily waived and the confidentiality of the communications must be jealously guarded. The importance of protecting these privileges and guarding against their waiver is heightened where the company has already commenced an internal investigation as to matters likely within the scope of the warrant, as there may very well exist highly confidential written communications between attorney and client about the very matters that are now under government investigation.

Effort must be made immediately at the scene of the search to disclose to the agents the existence of privileged materials on computer drives or in files. Those communications with the agents need to be promptly documented and, if those warnings have not deterred the agents, the types of privileged documents that were likely seized should be catalogued so that appropriate relief can be obtained by company counsel, if necessary. Obviously, if an internal investigation by the business has already been launched before the government search, resulting in the company's files containing interview materials and communications with counsel, effort should be made to urge the agents to simply set those identifiable files aside pending a negotiated pre-seizure review process agreed to by the prosecuting attorney and counsel.

When agents during the course of a search believe themselves nonetheless authorized to seize non-privileged materials that might be contained in the company's *legal files*, the government ordinarily assembles a *"taint team"* to identify any non-privileged material subject to seizure under the terms of the warrant. The agents on that team will typically have been instructed to review cursorily only the headings of file folders or the captions of documents to ascertain whether there is likely to be privileged (and relevant) material in the files. It is important that these activities be closely monitored. In such sensitive circumstances, the agents involved often will permit counsel and/ or senior management to be present to observe the procedures employed by them to prevent the inadvertent seizure of privileged materials and to prevent against later claims that there was wholesale rummaging through legal files.

Monitoring the Activities of the Agents

It may prove important in later court proceedings that the company contemporaneously documented how the agents executed a warrant. For example, if it appears that agents seized files on a wholesale basis for their convenience, or that they indiscriminately seized computers and servers without making even a minimal effort to determine that documents or data authorized to be seized were located thereon, the company's attorneys might later have a basis to file a motion for return of property or to suppress evidence. The company's representatives and employees need to remain observant during the search and to document in writing any seemingly irregular activity. Importantly, employees who have reported any unusual, hostile or inappropriate conduct or comments by the agents should be interviewed by counsel as soon as practicable. Because it will be extremely difficult for a lay-manager or even for in-house counsel to predict accurately what might be of later significance to a court, the better course is to document even the slightest irregularity for later review by counsel.

In many countries in Europe and Asia, companies have significant legal right to monitor the work of the searching authorities as well as to object on the scene to the way the search is being conducted (and even to limit what is taken without copying). In the United States, there are no such rules and a company's ability to observe the manner in which a warrant is being executed depends largely on the attitude of the lead case agent on the scene. There is never any harm, once things have calmed and the search is underway, to ask that designated employees be allowed to observe and witness the searches being conducted. Much will depend on the agent's assessment of the government's ability to go about the search in an orderly fashion, with minimal disruption or distraction, and without risk that the agents will lose the ability physically to control the areas being searched. Often the agents will not object, particularly if there is no security risk and the observing employees are unobtrusive. If company personnel are in a position to do so, detailed notes should be made of the progression of the search.

Computer Search Issues: Protecting Privileged and Proprietary Data

Perhaps the most intrusive thing the government can do is seize computer servers and take away from a business work station computers and the laptops of corporate executives and their assistants. Computer search issues present to the company – and to prosecutors and the courts for that matter – difficult legal and pragmatic concerns. Not the least of these is the fact that, because of the prolific business use of email to communicate even highly sensitive information, the computers often contain confidential communications between counsel and client as well as proprietary and trade secret information.

The issue of computer searches provides for company counsel the greatest opportunity to negotiate limitations of a search with the agents on the scene or with the prosecutor. Often, when computers and servers are to be seized, the agents will have on their search team designated IT-trained agents responsible specifically for conducting the computer searches. Counsel for a business, in order to negotiate with the agents regarding the scope and intrusiveness of these computer searches or seizures, will need access to the company's IT professionals to obtain a quick understanding of the systems and databases involved. The IT team should also be enlisted to at least observe what the agents are doing with the systems.

There will be a not insignificant chance that the government will, in response to counsel's plea that seizure of computers will injure the business, allow computer workstations and systems to remain operational and in place while the company makes arrangements for hardware replacements or to "*mirror image*" copies of the hard drives sought to be seized. At other times, the government may be content to make their own mirror image copies of computers and data servers while at the scene and to leave with only a copy. Agents may also peruse individual laptops or desktop computers to determine generally the operating or email systems being used or the association of a computer to a specific person. Rarely, however, will government agents sit in front of terminals at the business being searched and conduct searches for specific data. The government more typically will, if interested in the contents of a particular hard drive, seize first and subject it to a later search using forensic tools at the law enforcement agency. When that happens a hard drive or computer might be held for as long as 30-45 days before being returned. Of course, because the removal of computers or business equipment for *any* period of time, however brief, can negatively impact operations, the company should not hesitate to propose reasonable alternatives to the government's simply taking equipment away. If the business fails to convince the government not to take computers and equipment necessary to the business, an application to the court may be made after the search has concluded for their expedited return. Rarely, however, is there time or ability to petition the issuing court to stop their seizure entirely based simply on the business disruption occasioned by the seizures.

After the fact, post-search protection of proprietary data and trade secrets seized by the government is relatively easily dealt with, as a court can later fashion a confidentiality order and otherwise protect against public dissemination of the information obtained by the government. These sorts of orders are granted by the courts daily in civil cases and if data being searched contains highly proprietary or trade secret information the agents on the scene and counsel should be so informed. The government will likely not stop its search and might not even be required by a court to return all such data after the search, but the courts can prohibit the government from sharing the data with competitors and witnesses, or from otherwise disclosing it to the public.

However, as to the communications between counsel and client regarding matters that might be reasonably related to the government's investigation, the ability of a court retrospectively to remedy the consequences of the agents' receipt and use of privileged material is much more limited. If the government has unreasonably insisted that critical servers or individual computers containing attorney-client privileged materials be seized without delay, emergency application to the court issuing the warrant may be necessary. Such a motion, beyond seeking to prevent the physical confiscation of servers or laptops, may request alternatively that the court order that items taken during the search be reviewed first by a Special Master to prevent the disclosure of legally privileged attorney-client and attorney work product materials to the investigators. Likewise, if it appears more generally that agents have seized materials in apparent disregard of or indifference to the admonition that attorney-client materials are contained in files or databases, company counsel may decide there to be a sufficient basis to prepare a motion for the immediate return of the property seized. It is not likely that a court will order wholesale return of such materials, but there may be opportunity to assure that precautions have been taken to protect from government view things that are not legally appropriately subject to the review of a prosecutor or agents investigating a company or its employees.

The Department of Justice has circulated detailed memoranda regarding the legal issues involved in computer searches and seizures. While any law enforcement search of a business will have been an unusual and extraordinary event for the company, the government's computer search protocols and processes are well established and understood by agents in the field. Most issues of concern to a business relating to seizures of its computers have been addressed before by the agents in other cases, and typically they are resolved with an eye towards the minimization of the risk of business disruption. It is important to engage the agents as to these issues – and to do so calmly and reasonably.

The Aftermath: Putting the Pieces Back Together

The effects of the government's execution of a search warrant at a place of business will usually be felt by the company for days, weeks and sometimes even months. There are important tasks that the company must attend to without delay in the days immediately following the event.

Preparing a Post-Search Inventory

The agents at the scene of the search are required, at its conclusion, to complete and leave an inventory of the items seized. This is often referred to as the "*return*" because it is the record that, by law, must be delivered, or *returned*, to the judge or magistrate that has issued the warrant. The business should not rely on the agents' delivery of the return as a substitution for its own inventory of the items to be seized. The government's inventory will likely be very cursory (it may identify documents seized only by file cabinet or file drawer labels). Immediately after the search someone should be assigned to take that cursory inventory and supplement it with a more precise accounting of the items actually seized.

Not infrequently, because the execution of a search warrant is the first overt sign that the government is investigating a business, the investigation may take many months if not years after the search was done to conclude. The agents are likely to want to keep the entirety of the fruits of their search throughout the pendency of the investigation and they have no general obligation at law to make copies of materials that have been seized. The federal rules of criminal procedure permit a person or company that has been subject to a search to petition a court to order that certain property taken be returned to it. Promptly completing the inventory of items taken that are important to the functioning of the business, as well as documenting instances during which the agent's seizures appeared excessive and inappropriate, may be critical to the success of such a motion.

Dealing with the Media

There is no secrecy attending to the government's execution of a warrant. Warrants are, as we have noted, executed during business hours and by agents wearing raid jackets. Imagine the all-too-recurring scenario where local television cameras have captured video of agents carting off box after box of records as well as computers, laptops, work stations and servers from a business. Frame after frame, the cameras are witnessing "*the police*" placing such things on the back of a truck and hauled away. Often, the initial reaction by a company to the resulting media inquiries will be to fashion some statement minimizing the expected impact of the search, and of the investigation that prompted it. The company is going to want to do more, though, to defend itself publicly, to include making broad declarations of its innocence.

The best advice is to refrain from making any immediate response to media inquiries beyond one that initially and calmly expresses the company's cooperation with law enforcement. Comment about the investigation itself, and as to its expected progress, duration and outcome, are to be avoided. Not infrequently the business will have little idea regarding the precise scope and direction of an investigation and the least said often is the best option as poorly delivered communications -- including broad denials of wrongdoing -- can have a profoundly negative impact upon the attitude and perceptions of government investigators. If a comment is required, counsel can help the business avoid making declarations that may later prove troublesome. Overall, work in earnest will need to begin regarding a comprehensive communications strategy, and not infrequently communications consultants are enlisted to help manage the crisis these events sometimes prompt.

Addressing Employees, Shareholders, Regulators and Others

The business will also find itself, in the immediate aftermath of a search, faced with the question of what specifically ought to be disclosed to directors, shareholders, investors, creditors, suppliers and employees. And, beyond the acute institutional pressures on a business to communicate publicly, the government's execution of a warrant – and the reasons underlying it – may implicate U.S. securities law disclosure obligations for a publicly-traded company. To the extent that the business operates in a highly regulated industry, the execution of a search warrant is likely as well to generate interest and inquiries by federal and state regulators, which if left unaddressed may prompt the opening of separate but "parallel" regulatory investigations.

There will, then, be times when management will absolutely have to say something about the matter. Little succinct advice or best practice exists here, beyond that: (a) just as with the fashioning of media statements, even quiet protestations to constituents of the company's innocence can come back to haunt a company unaware of precisely what evidence of wrongdoing the government has that led it to seek the warrant; (b) it is never a good idea to belittle or dismiss the government's interest in the business or to in any way indicate hostility to the government's work; and (c) in all such circumstances the company should proceed with caution and with the active assistance of counsel.

Chapter 3

Law Enforcement Interviews of Senior Management and Lower Level Employees

Perhaps the most critical phase of any government investigation of corporate misconduct is the interview of employees suspected of having knowledge of the conduct of others who are actively under investigation, and ultimately of the persons themselves suspected of being complicit in a scheme. Much preparation by the government goes into these interviews. Particularly in the investigation of *white-collar* business crimes, significant witness interviews by the government will usually occur only after documents have been obtained and comprehensively reviewed, after a cooperator or other insider or whistleblower has been exhaustively debriefed, and after preliminary interviews of lower level personnel have been completed. Considerable attention is usually given by the government to the sequencing of these more important interviews in such a way as to build up to the witnesses the government may suspect either to have a motive to lie or deflect or to have been complicit. The well-prepared agent or prosecutor will have documents and the accounts of other witnesses at hand, and a full understanding of the chronology of events, so as confront the errant witness when and if testimony begins to wander.

For most employees asked to sit for a law enforcement interview, the event will not require any extraordinary attention or forethought. However, for the manager under whose watch misconduct is alleged to have occurred, or for the employee who suspects that his or her conduct may be under scrutiny, the prospect of being interviewed can be terrifying. Questions will swirl: *"What are my rights?," "Do I even have to meet with the agents?," 'Should I get a lawyer?," " Will the government think I'm guilty if I ask to have a lawyer with me?," "What will the company think if I ask for a lawyer?," "What will the company think if I decide not to sit down with the agents?," "How should I prepare for this?," "What happens if I can't remember something correctly, can I stop the interview?"* Plainly the employee-witness needs help to sort these issues out. But the company's own attorney is probably not the best person to answer these questions and hiring a lawyer will be expensive.

We address in this Chapter the limits of what a responsible business can and should do, consistent with the company's own independent interest in cooperating with the government and in punishing errant employees, to assist its employees and managers who have been asked by the government to be interviewed. Potential conflicts of interest – between the interests of the company on the one hand and the interests of the employee or manager on the other – will often abound, many times disqualifying the company's lawyers from doing much directly for the employee. We describe below how most businesses embroiled in government investigations manage to reconcile these competing interests.

A Hypothetical -- The *"Drop In"* Interview

Consider for purposes of the discussion below the following scenario:

During the weekend, a regional west coast newspaper published the first in a planned series of four articles regarding your high-flying Genetics Division. It had appeared from initial reports received from persons interviewed by the paper that the focus of the articles was going to be unrelated to the document requests the government had made last year that had suggested the possibility that there might have been significant improper billing of lab tests by the Genetics Division. Rather, it seemed that the stories were going to focus on some of the lavish spending and personal idiosyncrasies of the Division's founder (only recently moved to an executive position at the company's east coast headquarters and appointed to the Board of Director's Audit

Committee). Other newspapers had in the past reported on the colorful antics of the executive, but you were still concerned that the reporters would learn of the lab testing questions, since the VA-OIG document demands were a poorly kept secret within the Division.

To your surprise, the subject of the first article was an entirely new subject – the report that the Genetics Division had, in the two years prior to your company's acquisition, awarded $100s of thousands of business through consulting and marketing contracts to friends and associates of a local County Health Department Commissioner. The Commissioner, who was still in office, has had a long personal relationship with your Genetics Division founder and was in a position to influence the award of not just grants but a very significant procurement contract Genetics had landed with a major metropolitan research hospital relating to an experimental treatment protocol.

While you are unaware of any improprieties, you certainly know that the financial controls at the Genetics Division were never as tight as you would have liked them to have been. Nothing untoward had been identified during the pre-acquisition due diligence conducted two years ago, but you know that during the last company year-end audit your auditors had brought to your attention several large invoices issued by a Genetics Division consultant that contained entries reported as suspicious. The invoices were significant enough that you had been asked, as a matter of corporate policy, to review and approve them before payment – which you had done. For reasons unknown to you, your auditors seemed to have dropped their interest in the invoices and no mention was made of it in the audit report. Still, the invoices had worried you for months and, after reading the weekend news reports, you wondered if you had dropped the ball by not pursuing the issue further.

It is Monday morning and your head is full of thoughts as to what you should do next. As you leave your house and approach your car, two young and well-dressed men walk up to you, discretely display identification, tell you they are with the FBI, and ask if you would not mind answering a few questions. Knowing you have done nothing wrong, you agree. They suggest you accompany them to their car, an unmarked sedan, and come with them to the local FBI office. This time you pause, at least mentally, and then only momentarily.

The surprise of the encounter has you walking with the agents to the car, although you are worried about your appointments that morning.

The agents are professional, very courteous and attempt to make small talk. Finally, you begin better to process the situation and wonder whether you have any reason to be concerned. You are unaware of what the agents want to speak to you about. The connections with the Health Commissioner? Last year's Medicare billing questions? The suspicious invoices? "Maybe," you think, "I better call my General Counsel and find out what I should do."

You ask one of the agents whether it would make sense to have the interview later in the day so you can talk to a lawyer. The agent does not seem surprised with your question, and says simply, "We can do that." But he then immediately asks you, "Do you think you need a lawyer?" He assures you the conversation should only take 30 minutes or so, and that he thought it was particularly important that you take advantage of the opportunity that was being presented to you now. The last comment sounds more than a little ominous. You are uncertain as to what you should do, but you certainly do not want to signal to the agents that you believe you have anything to hide. You worry that if you insist on having a lawyer present the agents will think that you have done something wrong. It's important they know right away you are innocent.

You tell the agents you need to call the office to re-arrange a 9:30 a.m. staff meeting. They do not object and upon your call your assistant advises that the Genetics Division CFO had just within minutes called for you. The Division CFO said it was very urgent that he talk to you at your first opportunity. You wonder whether the FBI was interviewing others.

A business facing a government investigation into the conduct of its employees will almost invariably pledge its full cooperation very early on, and will often be eager to be involved in facilitating government requests for employee interviews. A business for obvious reasons cannot much afford to appear to resist an official investigation of the bad conduct of employees or be hostile to its ends. Yet, what about the personal interests of the company's employees?

They are going to be on the front line of the investigation. A company can be fined and suffer all kinds of negative financial consequences for the misconduct of employees, but it is not going to jail.

Government investigations of corporations can thrust upon employees and their employer hard to reconcile concerns. For its part, the company will look out for itself, cooperate with the government and punish or fire wrongdoers. Yet the company is not going to just throw employees *"under the bus"* –– in fact, in many cases there may be a legal duty to provide employees with the help of a lawyer or to fund a defense against future charges. Even if there is no legal duty to do so, a company is likely going to want to stand by its employees for the sake of maintaining morale and good order –– at least until there is proof of actual wrongdoing. A premature termination or suspension of an employee is going to be ill-perceived within the company and as motivated by a *"corporate"* interest to curry favor with the government. On the other hand, keeping an errant employee on full pay status is potentially to be seen by the government as motivated by a desire to buy silence and loyalty.

For their part, employees will understand themselves obligated to cooperate fully and tell the truth to investigators. There will also, however, be the natural instinct for employees not only to protect themselves personally but to avoid being forced unnecessarily to *"snitch"* on colleagues or friends or otherwise get the company in trouble. A senior manager might particularly feel caught in between, knowing that he or she will be expected by the company also to cooperate without hesitation and sit for an interview, notwithstanding nagging anxiety that he or she might actually have personal exposure.

Resolution of the harder questions – such as whether the company should suspend an employee or instead pay for lawyers for its employees, or whether employee witnesses should be asking for immunity before sitting with the government – typically require guidance by counsel. But in-house or outside counsel cannot be asked to help everybody – the company, management, the Board, employees. The lawyer would have to try to balance far too many potentially competing interests. How then best to help all parties who have a personal or business interest in the outcome of the government investigation?

Anticipating the possible commencement of a law enforcement investigative interview program prompts numerous questions important not only to a business, but to its management and employees likely to be of interest to the government:

Do the agents have the right to speak to employee witnesses about company business without company counsel being present?

When can a company's General Counsel or outside corporate or litigation counsel appropriately undertake to represent both the company and individual employees?

Conversely stated, when should the company arrange for managers and employees to have separate counsel? Who pays for this?

If separate counsel is obtained for one or more employees or managers, are there ways in which your company counsel can keep abreast of what is happening with respect to government's communications with that employee? Or as to the status of the employee in the government's investigation?

What about lower level employees? Do each of them require separate counsel or can the company get one lawyer to represent them all? Does the company need to get them attorneys at all?

What should the company tell employees about the possibility that law enforcement personnel may wish to speak to them?

And what of the interest of the employee or manager that is being asked to submit to an interview? Should he or she, as a personal matter, submit to an interview without having counsel present? Can he or she, practically speaking, request the presence of counsel without adverse consequence?

Can a business punish an employee who does not cooperate with government investigators?

Can an employee, given the company's pledge of "*complete cooperation*," as a practical matter decline entirely the invitation to speak to agents? What are the protections available to an employee to avoid incriminating him or herself?

What information and assurances can counsel get from investigators in order to protect (and calm) his or her client, whether it be the company or an employee or manager?

Who Represents the Employees?

The extent to which a company's lawyers may properly represent both the company and its employees in dealing with the government is an important issue in any investigation. Because rules governing the legal profession limit the ability of lawyers to represent multiple clients who have substantially competing personal and business interests at stake, a company often has to grapple with how best to assist members of management and lower level employees who may unexpectedly find themselves the subject of the government's attention.

Worst case, the issue is thrust on everyone suddenly, requiring exigent resolution. In fast developing investigations, where it appears that government agents are in fact fanning out simultaneously to speak to numerous employees without the company having had warning of the investigation, prosecutors not infrequently receive telephone calls from counsel for the business in which counsel claims to represent the company, its management *and* its employees. In that call, the company's lawyer may also ask that the agents go through the lawyer to set up future interviews. And, if company counsel truly represented each and every one of the employee-witnesses, the government lawyers leading the investigation team would have to honor the request. That is because legal rules require that lawyers not speak directly to a potential witness represented by another lawyer without the witness's lawyer being present.

Two questions present themselves: First, does the company's lawyer ever actually represent "*all employees*"? Second, is it proper from an ethical standpoint for the lawyer to represent numerous persons having potentially competing interests at stake?

To the first question, the answer is in most cases, "*No.*" The law requires that any individual know and consent to a lawyer's representation. It is not enough for company counsel to say, "*The investigation is about our company, I represent the company and have been asked by the company to represent all of its employees.*" The law measures the formation and scope of an attorney-client relationship on a person-by-person and entity-by-entity basis. The supposed client in this case (the individual employee who has been asked by the government to be interviewed) must have voluntarily entered into an attorney-client relationship with the lawyer. Since the company's lawyer has not spoken to *"all employees"* and gotten their approval to be represented by the company's lawyer, the lawyer cannot claim to represent the employee. We note one caveat – if the employee is a manager with sufficient status and authority in the company so as to be deemed to be in a position to speak for the company (the lawyer's true client), or to act or *"bind"* the company as to the expected area of inquiry, the company's attorney may have the right to be involved in any communication between government prosecutors and the employee or executive about those subjects. The government cannot on its own directly speak to *"the company"* where the company is represented by counsel -- a senior manager with authority to speak for the company is going to viewed as personifying the company and thus not approachable outside the presence of company counsel. Even there, however, the company's lawyer does not directly represent any interest of the executive in his personal and individual capacity – company counsel will be there only to protect the company. Bottom line, blanket claims by a lawyer to represent all employees without having first spoken to each of the employees generally do not work.

To the second question, the answer is, *"Maybe."* It is permissible for a lawyer to represent multiple clients as to one matter. But, for a lawyer to represent multiple parties having potentially conflicting interests, not only must all parties to the arrangement agree to it but the potential conflicts must be of a nature that they can actually be reconciled. Counsel for the company might here ask, *"If the corporation and all of its employees, managers and directors are all innocent of wrong-doing, as I know them to be, aren't their interests perfectly aligned? Where is the conflict of interest that requires us to go out and hire a lot of attorneys for them?"* However, counsel for the company is never going to know for a certainty – without being a mind reader – whether an individual employee possesses information harmful to the employee or to the company or to a very senior executive or colleague. An employee in the possession of information highly damaging to the company or to a senior executive may in fact be eager to speak to the government without the company's lawyer being present. Conversely, the wayward employee may not wish to talk to the government – or even to company counsel for that matter – in circumstances in which that the company and its lawyers have pledged the company's full cooperation. It is unfair to the witnesses in either of these circumstances for the company's lawyer to be involved in the witnesses' interactions with the government. A lawyer's multiple representation of the company and *"all employees"* is thus more often than not simply impracticable.

Consider the consequences of company counsel's making the wrong call as to whether he or she may represent both employee-witnesses and the company. Representation of the manager who eventually confesses to the lawyer the untruth of an initial protestation of innocence communicated to the government in an early witness interview presents to the lawyer a clear dilemma. Clearly, one of the lawyer's clients, the company, has an interest in reducing its own financial exposure and harms to its business reputation; it has an interest in punishing an errant employee; it has an interest in fully cooperating with the government and mitigating the consequence of bad employee conduct. But what of the lawyer's other client, the manager? What does the attorney advise the manager to do? Decline to talk to the government agents and face possible charges? Come clean, confess that he or she lied? Attempt to obtain leniency by cooperating against other corporate wrongdoers, to include the company itself or senior executives?

Thus, with limited exception, the better and usual course – to avoid ethical issues as well as to assure the investigators that the business will not interfere in the investigative processes – is to engage separate counsel for each member of senior management having any significant investigative interest to the government.

As to lower level employees, unless there is a basis to believe that individual lower level employees are complicit or will have conflicting interests between themselves, a business may appropriately arrange to retain one or more independent *"pool counsel"* – separate from company counsel – to represent all lower level employees who desire (and ask for) representation. *Pool counsel*, in turn, will be watchful for any conflict situations that may unexpectedly arise requiring the appointment of a separate attorney for an individual within the pool. Conceivably, as well, smaller groups of mid-level managers might be represented by one counsel together (again, separate from the company's lawyer), but the possibility of the later occurrence of an actual conflict of the interests between one or more managers increases with the number of managers represented.

It sounds expensive. It is. Still, it is the usual practice of companies to undertake to arrange and pay for separate counsel for employees and managers who are close to the matters being investigated and who thus should be represented separately. The alternative – making managers and employees fend for themselves and get their own lawyers at their own expense if they want one – can easily prove pennywise and pound foolish. There is much value to the company in ensuring the orderly progress of an investigation, and of having its employees making smart choices about how they deal with the government.

Ultimately, even if a business were disinclined to provide and pay for counsel for a manager approached by the government to be interviewed, the refusal to help the manager retain a lawyer may not even be an option – corporate by-laws or the indemnification laws in the state of employment might in fact legally require the retention of counsel, and the advancement of legal fees, subject to a right to recoup those costs if there is a criminal conviction. Counsel should be consulted as to the indemnification obligations of a company to its managers and employees.

Finally, the fact that a company has decided to pay the legal fees of counsel for an individual manager or for a *pooled* class of employees does not in and of itself create a conflict of interest for the attorney who agrees to accept such an engagement. The law permits a third party to pay a lawyer's professional fees connected with the representation of a client other than the payer, provided that there is appropriate disclosure to the client and further that the employee-client agrees to that party's assumption of the costs. Even when the company pays for an independent lawyer for the client, the lawyer's duty is always to the client – the attorney cannot be asked by the company to betray the employee's confidences with the lawyer or otherwise compromise the interests of the employee or manager because the company paid for the services of the lawyer.

The Joint Defense Agreement

How does the business, then, maintain control over the company's overall response to an investigation if all these lawyers are in the picture representing individual managers? *It does not.* The reason why separate counsel for individuals is usually required is to ensure that the business does not deliberately or inadvertently interfere with or control conduct or decisions that necessarily have to be made by the individuals themselves, for their own reasons, without regard necessarily to the interests of the company.

Nonetheless, attorneys representing companies and those that represent employees often find it in the mutual best interest of their clients that the lawyers speak freely and candidly with each other about an investigation, as well as share confidential and sensitive information, provided that it is pursuant to an understanding that the information shared between the lawyers will not in turn be disclosed to others or to the government. It is not unusual in these circumstances to see counsel agree among themselves formally and in writing (but with the explicit consent of their clients) to share confidential and sometimes legally privileged information subject to the further understanding that the sharing of the information between them will not result in a waiver of the attorney-client privilege or abandonment of the confidential nature of the information shared. Such agreements – coined *"joint defense agreements"* – are common in complex white-collar criminal investigations.

Counsel representing a company that has arranged for separate counsel for individual managers or employees will at times be a participant in such a joint defense undertaking, even if only to a limited extent – it is particularly in the company's interest to understand not just the progression of an investigation but the facts underlying the government's work. An early decision to hire separate counsel for an individual manager may effectively cut off the company's lawyer's access to information in the possession of the independently represented manager or employee. A joint defense agreement permits company counsel – and counsel for the individuals – to share and have continued access to information of interest to all while preserving its confidentiality.

Joint defense agreements are controversial.

On the one hand, viewed most benignly, joint defense agreements allow clients to make better-informed decisions – counsel and client are better informed about the facts, better informed about the direction and scope of the government's interest and better informed about the relative risk of proceeding in one direction over another. From the government's standpoint even, the information obtained by a lawyer-participant in a joint defense agreement often helps inform an individual client in deciding whether to cooperate and enter a negotiated guilty plea – and the company to realize whether it has true exposure requiring it quickly to come to terms with the government.

On the other hand, many prosecutors do not understand the utility and motivations behind joint defense agreements. Some view them suspiciously as a means for lawyers to effectively conspire to keep witnesses of potential value quiet so as not to implicate others. To them, these agreements look simply like an effort by defense lawyers to *"circle the wagons"* and protect the guilty. It is for that reason that many defense practitioners prefer not to memorialize the understandings in writing.

However, the courts generally recognize and enforce joint defense agreements in the criminal defense context. Ultimately, these agreements do not generally pose the types of obstacles to the prompt resolution of criminal actions that many prosecutors imagine. If poorly drafted, however, a *"JDA"* may actually be used offensively by an individual participant in the arrangement to limit or challenge entirely the government's use at trial of testimony from a former member of the agreement. Questions will also arise regarding the ability of a lawyer for a charged defendant to impeach and aggressively cross-examine a now-cooperating government witness (and former *JDA* participant) when he or she appears at trial using, when challenging the witness, confidential information earlier obtained from that witness' lawyer through the joint defense agreement. It is incumbent on counsel for an employee who conceivably might later decide to withdraw from such an arrangement (which almost by definition is every participant to a *JDA*) to make sure that the agreement is drafted in such a way as to permit his or her client to cooperate with the government without encumbrance. In addition, responsible counsel representing a participant in a *JDA* will be careful only to share so much information with other counsel as actually serves the interests of his or her client. There is usually no need for an attorney to disclose to other attorneys participating in the *JDA* intimate details of his or her client's involvement in an alleged scheme. Likewise, ethical and responsible counsel will independently advise his or her client to abandon any joint defense undertaking if it is truly not in the client's best interest to continue to participate in the agreement. Written joint defense agreements specifically contemplate this scenario and provide the manner and means by which a participant can withdraw from a *JDA* and enter a plea and cooperation agreement with the government, and even testify against former co-participants in the *JDA*, without compromising the privileged and continuing confidential nature of information that had been previously shared with the lawyer of the now-withdrawn participant.

As for a company's involvement in a *JDA*, the risk of government misperception needs to be considered carefully. Generally speaking, the government will more often encounter joint defense agreements entered into by lawyers for company employees without involvement of counsel the company, as the company's becoming a party may significantly impair the company's ability to later provide the government with a complete and full report of facts found during the company's internal investigation. The government will expect that a company will cooperate with the government and provide information free of any self-imposed limitations on information sharing. Still, there are ways for the lawyer for a business to be involved in a *JDA* without compromising the company's ability to fully cooperate with the government. Counsel for all participants simply need to be particularly circumspect as to the information that gets shared. Ultimately, the question of whether counsel for an individual or for the company should enter into a joint defense understanding is a matter that will require considerable discussion and deliberation between counsel and client.

Starting at the Beginning: Does the Employee or Manager Even Need Counsel?

A company, and indeed many employees themselves, may not see the need for employees to have a lawyer present when the government interviews them.

We think, though, that it is ordinarily best for a company to make available to all employees some form of legal assistance if the employee wishes it. The consequences of an uninformed employee not addressing the encounter with the government soberly enough, with the right orientation and honestly, can be monumental. An employee who decides in the middle of an interview to mislead or outright lie in order to cover for a fellow employee or boss that the employee suddenly realizes is at risk will likely him or herself later suffer a lot of heartache and trouble when the government appreciates that the witness was less than candid.

Experience has shown that when a company advises its employees that independent counsel has been retained and is available to be consulted in advance of any scheduled government interview, most employees — if driven only by curiosity or by a need to relieve anxiety over the impending encounter with "*law enforcement*" — will contact counsel and discuss the matter. The job of the attorney is straightforward. Counsel will size up the employee's involvement in the matter being investigated and advise the employee of any perceived risks and of his or her rights as a witness in the investigation. Counsel will be looking for any indication that the employee may have in any way furthered the scheme, by facilitating its commission, by failing timely to report evidence of it, or by later helping to conceal bad conduct by superiors or co-workers. And, of course, as the government moves up the organizational ladder to talk to supervisors and mid-level managers, counsel will appreciate that the chances that the employee may him or herself be of direct investigative interest are increased. The value of counsel here is largely in counsel's ability to appropriately assess the risk to the employee or manager.

Competent and experienced counsel will advise the represented employee that, while the decision to go forward with the interview lies entirely with the employee, if the employee sits with the agents for an interview, he or she must scrupulously tell the truth. Counsel will also, even if believing the employee to have nothing to be worried about, usually offer to sit with the employee during the interview so as to watch for anything unusual that might affect counsel's conclusion that the witness has little reason for concern. There is nothing inappropriate for a witness -- even one with knowledge of facts likely to be only of peripheral interest to the government or one who believes not to have done anything wrong -- to bring a lawyer to a government interview session.

Consider the hypothetical we outlined above. Should our manager overcome his or her legitimate concerns about creating an adverse appearance in the minds of the agents and about unnecessarily inconveniencing them, by simply insisting upon having the ability to consult with and to be accompanied by counsel during the interview? Almost invariably the better course is to do so. Why? A meeting with an FBI agent, a regulator, a policeman or a prosecutor is often, for the witness, an unusual life event, not likely to recur, and one that can actually be fraught with peril. Missteps during an interview may be seen as an effort to obstruct the investigation – itself a crime. And by design, these interviews are intended to be conducted without much said by the government about the scope of its investigation and certainly without identification of the persons the government suspects to have done something wrong. Even when an agent makes assurances that, in his or her view, the witness has *nothing to be worried about*," it is simply wise to have a detached, objective observer with the employee, one who can allay the anxieties normally accompanying such an encounter and one who can help memorialize the interview by good notetaking.

The adverse inference the witness thinks might be drawn by the agents from a request to confer with or otherwise get the assistance of a lawyer is usually not drawn at all. Agents and prosecutors are accustomed to having counsel present at interviews of witnesses, even witnesses who are innocent and have nothing whatever to worry about. And there usually is not, in an investigation of business crimes, the sort of exigencies suggested by an agent anxious to get an interview done. These investigations take time. Agents and prosecutors are used to having to schedule interviews around the availability of counsel. The employee, then, is often well-advised to politely -- but persistently -- ask the agent for an opportunity to speak to an attorney first.

Determining the Status of the Employee Client: "*Witness*," "*Subject*" or "*Target*"

Counsel approached by a prospective client who has been asked to be interviewed by the government in a significant white-collar investigation will soon speak to the agent or prosecutor assigned to the investigation and ask about the client's *status* in the matter. Ordinarily a prosecutor will inform counsel that the client is just a "*witness*," which to most is understood as an affirmative assurance that the employee is not under investigation and does not have anything to be worried about. Provided that the characterization appears consistent with the counsel's own assessment, and provided further that counsel has a good rapport with the prosecutor and trusts that assessment, counsel may well feel that the client needs no further protection beyond a letter or email to or from the prosecutor confirming the government's characterization of the employee as a witness. However, a client's being advised that one is just a witness is no guaranty whatever that that status will not later change as the prosecutor learns more about the matter. Accordingly, counsel's independent assessment of the witness' exposure remains critical.

If the government, on the other hand, suggests the witness is a "*subject*" or "*target*" of the investigation, the client has cause for concern.

Particularly when a prosecutor informs a client, or their attorney, that the client is or may become a "*target*," the client has had a very bad day. In prosecutor parlance, it means that the client is a "*putative defendant*" – that is, someone the prosecutor believes has committed a crime and who *will most likely* be indicted. While, generally speaking, prosecutors will not as a matter of policy seek to compel a target to appear before the grand jury and testify under oath, the government is not shy about asking an employee or manager generally suspected of misconduct to sit for an interview – and there is no affirmative obligation on the part of the government to warn the witness of its suspicions. Where the prosecutor advises a lawyer before the interview that the lawyer's client is or may soon become a target of an investigation, counsel has in one sense, for immediate purposes, no work to do at all. If the prosecutor is unprepared to work out appropriate terms governing the use of an interview (*i.e.*, immunity) or of an acceptable disposition of the criminal case (*i.e.*, a plea agreement), counsel is likely to advise the client to sit tight, do nothing and rely upon the Fifth Amendment privilege not to provide evidence against oneself.

If the prosecutor advises that the client is a *"subject,"* counsel has much work to do. In fact, this scenario is the most challenging for the client and lawyer. Characterizing the witness as a subject generally signals that the prosecutor is looking at the conduct of the witness, and that the employee is at least on the government's radar screen for possible prosecution. But it also means that the government is uncertain at that stage of the investigation as to whether the employee has criminal culpability. This *in-between* characterization requires counsel to have a much more intense series of conversations with both the prosecutor and the client to appropriately assess risk. A decision needs to be made whether the interview will happen at all – the client may actually want to talk to the government to clear the air. But in many cases, the risk will be too great of proceeding at all without some protection and the client will be so advised no matter the client's belief as to his or her innocence.

Note that the distinction between *subject* and *target* does not necessarily hold true for all government investigators. Many federal agents (as opposed to federal prosecutors), do not even use the term *target* – so if the agent tells a lawyer that a witness is a *subject,* that is tantamount to identifying the witness as a *target,* that is, someone the attorney can expect will get indicted. For these agents, most witnesses are in a very broad *no man's land,* somewhere between government perception of complete innocence (*witness*) and strong suspicion and presumption of guilt (*subject*). To compound matters, many agents will not even engage in a discussion about the status of a witness. All this underscores the need to have counsel experienced in criminal defense and familiar with local law enforcement agency practice involved in those pre-interview conversations with the government about the status of a witness in an investigation.

Protecting the *"At-Risk"* Witness: *"Use"* and *"Derivative Use"* Immunity

If the employee has some potential exposure but counsel believes that a *"debriefing"* by the prosecutor and agent will convince the government not to charge the employee or, if the employee is a target and counsel has determined that the employee has invaluable information that will convince the government to extend a highly favorable plea agreement, counsel may advise the client to consider meeting with the government and providing information during a "*proffer*" session under *immunity* protection.

What does immunity mean?

Every person has the fundamental constitutional right not to be forced by the government to provide testimony or evidence against him or herself. If the government wants to overcome a person's refusal to testify, a court may force, or "*compel*," that testimony to occur. However, there is a price to be paid by the government for that compelled testimony – the constitutional right not to be a witness against oneself requires that, if one is forced to testify, the government also must forfeit the right to use the words and information supplied against the witness. The witness must legally be *immunized* from later *uses* of the information against the witness.

Immunity does not come automatically. It must be requested by the witness being asked to testify. Except in a few states, the law assumes that if a witness speaks to the government without asking for immunity the witness waives the constitutional right against self-incrimination. Accordingly, part of the conversation between client and counsel regarding an impending interview session with the government will focus on whether the witness should be asking for immunity.

There are essentially four different forms of immunity protection, one of which will, generally speaking, never be offered by the government and two of which are only rarely given. The most common form of immunity extended by the government – used primarily when a witness's status remains uncertain – is even then only grudgingly extended.

* ***Transactional immunity***: This form immunity is a promise by the government that the witness will never be prosecuted (except possibly for perjury or obstruction of justice if the witness lies) for any offense discussed during the debriefing. The U.S. Constitution does not require a prosecutor who compels a witness' testimony to extend

to the witness "*transactional immunity.*" Rather, the courts have held that a more limited form of immunity – "*use immunity*," discussed below – is adequate to vindicate the constitutional protection against self-incrimination. Transactional immunity is very broad. The consequence to the government of discovering the commission of an unknown crime from a witness during his or her testimony under a grant of transactional immunity means that the witness can never be prosecuted for the offense. The protection is so broad that, by way of example, a witness in a securities fraud investigation questioned pursuant to a grant of transactional immunity who confesses to a remote murder will be protected against a later prosecution for the murder. A witness is immunized against prosecution for the *transaction* or *event* spoken about. The government will almost never offer witnesses this type of protection.

*   ***Informal "Direct and Derivative Use" Immunity***: When the government extends this form of immunity (*informally*, by way of a letter agreement as opposed to court order), the government commits that it will neither *use* the information and statements obtained from the witness "*directly*" or "*derivatively*" against the witness to obtain an indictment or as evidence of guilt at trial. That is, the government cannot make direct use of the statements made during the interview by putting an agent on the stand at a trial to say that, on the date of the interview, the witness-later-turned-defendant admitted one or more facts the government is now relying on to convict the witness of a crime. Importantly, it also means that the agent also cannot use the information derivatively. The government will be prohibited from taking the statements and information provided by the witness during the interview and using them "*indirectly*" as leads to develop ostensibly *independent* evidence of guilt. In other words, when extending "*use and derivative use*" immunity, the government assumes the heavy burden of proving, if the witness is later charged, that none of the evidence it intends to use in the prosecution of the witness was *derived* from – that is, developed or based upon – leads

or information obtained from the witness. This is a very powerful form of immunity because it requires the government essentially to prove a negative – that all of its evidence was obtained free from any government knowledge obtained from the witness. The government is usually very reluctant to extend this form of immunity protection as it frequently makes the later prosecution of the witness practically impossible.

* ***"Statutory Use" Immunity***: The U.S. Supreme Court has held that while a court may, on application of the U.S. government, override a witness' invocation of his or her Fifth Amendment right to remain silent, the constitution requires that the witness receive *"use and derivative use"* immunity described above. *"Statutory immunity"* differs from the *"informal"* immunity in that it can be extended only by a U.S. District Court and it binds the government in every U.S. jurisdiction. *Informal immunity*, extended by letter agreement, on the other hand, is usually thought to be more limited, as binding only the local prosecutor's office, and containing all manner of government-imposed limitations and conditions to the grant of immunity. Again, because mounting a successful prosecution against a witness is almost impossible after the grant of *use and derivative use* immunity, prosecutors rarely (but not always) refuse a request that the witness obtain *statutory* use immunity as a condition of providing information to the government.

* ***"Informal Direct Use" or "Proffer" Immunity***: This is sometimes colloquially referred to as *"queen for a day"* immunity. It is extended by letter agreement; is typically coupled with numerous scope limitations; usually binds only the prosecutor's office for that attorney's geographic jurisdiction, or *"district"*; and only restricts the prosecutors from using the information and the witness' words *"directly"* against the witness at a later occurring trial. The government is free to make any other indirect or derivative use of the information as it sees fit, including by developing other evidence by which it later seeks to convict the witness. Ordinarily, this is the only form of immunity that

the government will be prepared to extend to cover a *proffer* session between the government and an individual, arranged to permit the government accurately to gauge the person's involvement or participation in a scheme. In this circumstance, *proffer immunity* is used to permit the government more fully to assess counsel's assertion that the witness is not complicit and should not be charged. It is likely the only form of immunity to be extended to a subject or target of an investigation too. The purpose of a proffer in this latter circumstance is to give the government an opportunity to assess the value of information ultimately to be provided pursuant to a later cooperation agreement. This form of immunity permits the government to proceed with the de-briefing without an effective commitment not to prosecute, because it will be free to pursue any leads provided by the witness should the government not be satisfied with the account provided by the witness.

Advising a client as to the wisdom of participating in an interview, with or without immunity protection, can be an immensely challenging exercise and requires the lawyer -- and ultimately the client -- to exercise extremely well-informed judgment. It is one of the most important decisions an employee-witness might be called upon to make. This, of course, underscores the risk that company counsel, who has typically pledged the corporation's full cooperation with the government, will suffer a conflict of interest if also undertaking to advise an employee with respect to his or her immunity options.

Advising Employees as to their Right to Counsel

Businesses must exercise enormous care when advising employees of the existence of a government investigation; of the possibility that agents might wish to interview them; of employee rights, both to participate in interviews and to decline to be questioned; and of the availability of counsel to advise or represent the employees in any interview. Unless the message is carefully and clearly delivered, there is significant risk that employees will later report to the government that the messenger (an executive or company counsel, for example), said words understood to the effect that, *"We didn't do anything wrong,"* *"This will all blow over,"* *"You don't have to talk to the government,"* or worse, *"If you must talk, the company will get a lawyer to sit with you."* Accordingly, any written communication to an employee or group of employees about their right to consult with counsel should be drafted or closely vetted by the company's attorney. If the communication is verbalized, there should be a prepared script which should be followed without elaboration or deviation. It is far too easy for an employee to misinterpret such a communication as suggesting that the employee not cooperate, and reports back to the agents or prosecutors to that effect can have devastating impact.

Chapter 4

Regulatory Subpoenas and Grand Jury Practice: Compelling the Production of Documents and the Appearance and Testimony of Witnesses

The government has broad power to compel persons and businesses to produce records and to make explanations on the record under oath regarding their conduct or business practices. When it comes to the government's obtaining documentary proof, much of that evidence can be had through the issuance of subpoenas that look much like the subpoenas lawyers issue and serve on witnesses in garden variety civil lawsuits between private parties. There are different types of subpoenas. *"Administrative subpoenas"* and regulatory *"civil investigative demands"* operate much like court-issued civil subpoenas and we will address below a number of best practices that should be followed when responding to such a subpoena or government investigative demand for the production of documents. Our particular focus in this Chapter will, however, be on the government's use of an unusually potent investigative tool – the *grand jury subpoena* -- to gather physical evidence and to compel the appearance and testimony of witnesses.

The grand jury is one of the most powerful means the federal government has at its disposal to uncover evidence of criminal wrong-doing. The government and its investigative grand juries conduct their affairs together under a strictly-enforced judicial mandate of secrecy. A grand jury is broadly authorized to issue subpoenas calling for the production of documents, the gathering of physical evidence, and the appearance and testimony of witnesses. Unlike a subpoena issued in a civil case, no meaningful mechanism exists for a party served with a grand jury subpoena to challenge its scope or the relevancy of its requests, or to object to it because it is burdensome. Courts pay extreme deference to the work of grand juries and only on exceedingly rare occasion will a court involve itself in disputes relating to the grand jury's investigative processes. Failure by a person served with a grand jury subpoena adequately to abide by its terms, or efforts directed to third-persons to frustrate compliance with a grand jury investigation, may be a criminal offense – obstruction of justice. Indeed, once aware that a federal grand jury subpoena has been issued regarding a particular matter – and thus on notice and that a federal grand jury is investigating an issue – a person acts at his or her extreme peril by in any way, directly or indirectly, interfering with the investigation.

A Hypothetical -- *"You've Been Served,"* Implications and Responses

For purposes of discussion, assume the following:

After an initial round of interviews by the FBI of employees at your Genetics Division, everything had gone quiet. Your in-house counsel advised you at the time of the interviews that it appeared that the FBI agents were interested exclusively in the relationship between your Genetics Division founder and certain public officials on the west coast. While your principal outside law firm had had some early discussion with the local US Attorney's Office during which it was confirmed that the government had "opened a matter" on the company, the exchange with the prosecutor was not otherwise illuminating. The government declined to say who it was investigating, what the scope of the investigation was, or even if there was any timetable to resolving the inquiry. In the nine months since those interviews the investigation appeared entirely dormant. Until recently.

Two weeks ago, an employee of a competitor clinical lab quietly advised one of your sales representatives that his employer had received a federal grand jury subpoena and that the subpoena had caused a lot of anxiety. Apparently, the subpoena called for documents relating to the sort of "bundling" and "up coding" that appeared to have been the focus of the entirely separate VA-OIG regulatory demand received by your Genetics Division almost two years ago. The several calls you have made to your counterpart at the competitor lab have gone unanswered. Although the report of the existence of the subpoenas caused you and other members of your management team some consternation, your counsel thought that the subpoenas were part of a general, industry-wide investigation of billing practices.

Last week your banker informally advised your Controller that he was working on a response to a "government demand" for financial records relating to your company. The banker provided no further details and made it clear that he was not comfortable providing more information. This morning your company received a federal grand jury subpoena calling for the production of a full five years' worth of data relating to your Genetics Division billing of one very specialized form of molecular testing. Your Controller was also served with a subpoena calling for his personal appearance and testimony before the grand jury in two weeks. Upon your asking your IT department for help gathering the records and information demanded by the subpoena, you learn that coincidentally just three months ago a very similar request for records and data had been made by your Genetics Division CFO.

A company's initial receipt of a grand jury subpoena ordinarily prompts numerous questions and anxious telephone calls. Typically, there is little or no forewarning that a grand jury subpoena will be served and the implications of the subpoena are usually the subject of much speculation. The fact that an employee of a business has also received a subpoena calling for a personal appearance and testimony will prompt further concerns. Management will want to know if the issuance of the subpoenas means that the company itself or members of management are under investigation, whether the information being asked for is instead related to an industry-wide inquiry or, better yet, whether the underlying investigation relates entirely to the conduct of others outside the company. While any responsible corporation will immediately set out to gather and secure records demanded to be produced, an impression must also be made on all involved in the collection of such records that this is no ordinary subpoena and that strict compliance with its terms is critical. Some consideration must be had as to who should be involved in that process. Also, to the extent that compliance with the subpoena may be burdensome, a dialogue needs to be established with the prosecutor involved to either limit its scope or to extend the time or manner of production. That dialogue will usually provide counsel for the company with an opportunity – albeit sometimes limited – to explore with the government the direction and scope of the grand jury's work.

Service of a grand jury subpoena on a business will prompt a number of questions:

Under what authority are grand jury subpoenas issued?

What if any facts can a business assume simply by virtue of the grand jury's issuance of a subpoena?

To whom in the government can questions be presented regarding the implications of the subpoena? Will those questions be answered?

How does a grand jury work? Are the courts involved? Where does a grand jury hold sessions? Can a representative of the company watch any of its work?

What is the grand jury subpoena response process? How are burdensomeness, privilege and relevancy objections to the subpoena addressed?

Who should be involved in gathering records? Should the company suspend its normal document retention policies? If so, for how long?

When will a business know when the grand jury's work is done?

The Purposes, Functions and Operation of a Grand Jury

The basic operation and functions of the grand jury are consistent throughout the federal system. The grand jury is a body tasked principally with investigating crimes and determining at the end of the investigation whether or not persons should be charged with federal felony offenses. It has the power to command persons to appear before it and give testimony, to produce records, or both. When appropriate, at the end of an investigation, it will issue charging documents, referred to as "*indictments*," by which formal criminal proceedings are commenced against individuals. While every grand jury is empaneled by a federal court and given basic instruction by the court to guide its work, the courts do not get directly involved in the grand jury process. No judge sits in and presides over sessions of the grand jury. Indeed, as noted, the courts pay enormous deference to the work of the grand jury.

Federal prosecutors, working with law enforcement agents, initiate grand jury investigations in the first instance and effectively control the timing and scope of their work. And it is federal prosecutors, and not the grand jury, that will decide what charges should be considered for indictment and what charges will *not* be pursued. However, it is the federal grand jury itself that must vote on and approve charges presented to it by the government. That means that every person charged by indictment with a federal felony offense has had his or her case presented to a grand jury for decision. At that *charging* stage, the grand jury's task is to decide whether there is "*probable cause*" to believe that the crimes described in the indictment were committed by the persons identified there. Probable cause does not mean that the government has satisfied the grand jury that it has proof by a "*preponderance of the evidence*" (more than 50% likelihood) that the crimes were committed as charged. Rather, colloquially speaking, the grand jury must be convinced only that there are reasonable grounds to believe that the crimes charged more likely than not occurred as alleged by the government.

While this might seem a slim basis upon which to rest a federal prosecution, any prosecutor presenting a case to a federal grand jury for indictment will believe that the government has in its possession proof of guilt "*beyond a reasonable doubt*," the standard by which a conviction must be had. One reason why the government must have such proof at the time of indictment is because, upon indictment, the grand jury's functions as to that matter ends. The prosecutor cannot after indictment invoke the grand jury's authority to issue subpoenas for documents and to compel testimony so as to gather additional trial evidence. And it is because of that that the grand jury has broad pre-indictment investigative authority – the grand jury has the largely unreviewable right to subpoena even marginally relevant documents and to call persons from around the United States to appear before it and answer its questions. Its mission is simply to investigate crime and, consistent with its broad mandate, it has broad powers.

A grand jury is comprised of 23 persons. Its members are drawn from the community, and pre-qualified by a court much like trial jurors are selected. However, unlike trial panels that sit for a single trial, the grand jury sits for 18 months (with the possibility of a six-month extension). Accordingly, a grand jury may meet only once a week or once a month. At times the grand jury may be inactive and not meet at all for weeks. Frequently, and particularly in busier judicial districts, grand jurors are assigned to consider specialized types of cases emanating from different sections within the prosecutor's office (*e.g.,* frauds, corruption, narcotics, *etc.*). Although all 23 grand jurors do not need to be present at each session, a quorum of 12 is required and it takes a minimum of 16 members to approve an indictment (that is, "*to return a true bill*").

A grand jury's business and deliberations are by law secret. Grand jurors, and the agents and prosecutors who appear before them, are strictly prohibited from sharing information as to the testimony or documents obtained by the grand jury, the scope and nature of its investigations and anything to do with its deliberations. This court-enforced rule of strict secrecy extends even to prohibit prosecutors who appear before and work with grand juries from disclosing any *grand jury information* to state law enforcement personnel and federal regulators with whom the prosecution team ordinarily work. Transcripts of witness testimony are not public. However, non-government witnesses who appear before the grand jury and persons and companies who are served with subpoenas for documents are not bound by these rules. Anything a non-government grand jury witness observes while before the grand jury may be disclosed to the world. Still, it is not unusual for a prosecutor to ask a witness appearing before the grand jury voluntary to refrain from discussing what happened at the session.

A prosecutor will decide when to open an investigation with the grand jury. Typically, the government will have started its investigative work well before a matter is presented to the grand jury. At times, due a desire to continue to coordinate efforts with non-grand-jury-authorized federal regulators or state law enforcement officials as long as possible before the grand jury secrecy rules are implicated, the commencement of a grand jury's involvement in a government investigation will be delayed. Once the grand jury's powers are invoked, all such cooperation and sharing of information must end.

Although the grand jury *"issues"* subpoenas, the subpoena is in fact usually drafted in the name of the grand jury, signed, and later served by the prosecutor assigned to investigate the matter all without having obtained the advance permission of the grand jury at all. While the subpoena will call for the physical production of documents before the grand jury on a date it is scheduled to sit, often the prosecutor will also agree that the documents can be delivered to the agent or prosecutor at the prosecutor's office. Still, the documents must always ultimately be presented to the grand jury by the government. The agent or prosecutor will undertake physically to *"return"* the documents to the grand jury before the grand jury has finished its work.

Testimony is another matter altogether. While receipt of a grand jury subpoena might prompt counsel for the witness to contact the prosecutor and suggest the holding of an informal pre-grand-jury-appearance interview session at the U.S. Attorney's Office, live, sworn testimony compelled pursuant to a grand jury subpoena can only be given before the grand jury itself. A prosecutor may not through a grand jury subpoena force a witness to appear at his or her office to be interviewed.

Only authorized persons may appear before the grand jury – the prosecutor, a court reporter and witnesses. Attorneys for witnesses are not allowed to observe. Nor are law enforcement agents who are working with the prosecutor on the matter, unless they are there having been called as witnesses to testify. Because no judge or defense counsel attend the proceedings, witnesses effectively must answer questions without objection as to their form or relevancy. A witness may, however, ask the prosecutor for permission, before answering a question, to talk to his or her attorney, who will be allowed to be nearby, but always outside the grand jury room. Those discussions between grand jury witnesses and their counsel are liberally allowed by prosecutors, although they are supposed to be limited in purpose to legal questions about the protection of evidentiary privileges or concerning the witness's right not to incriminate his or herself.

During a grand jury's deliberations on an indictment, no one except the grand jurors is allowed to be present – neither the prosecutor nor the court reporter assigned to the matter can witness the deliberative work of the grand jury. Should a grand jury approve the charges and return a *"true bill,"* the grand jury is taken before a federal magistrate, where the indictment is *"returned."* At that point, the grand jury's business is ended as to that matter. If the grand jury rejects the charges and returns a *"no true bill,"* the prosecutor still has the option to gather additional evidence and re-present the matter to the grand jury. However, because of the low standard of proof necessary to support an indictment (*probable cause*), and because of the ability of the prosecutor to get an early sense that the grand jurors may have a problem with a particular case, there is an extremely low incidence of grand juries declining to indict after being requested to do so by the government. Usually, in those rare cases, there is a unique proof problem with regard to the matter and the *no true bill* is the death of the case.

Because of the prominent role of prosecutors in the grand jury investigative and charging processes, some commentators criticize the system as unnecessarily dominated by the government. But the grand jury does in a very real way place citizens between the government and the charging of individuals with the commission of federal crimes. Members of the grand jury serve as an important check on the power of the government. Grand jurors also serve as a useful sounding board for the government in close cases. The requirement that, unless otherwise excused by the government, witnesses summonsed by the grand jury actually appear and testify before it under oath, is often helpful for a prosecutor looking to assess the credibility and effectiveness of witnesses the government will have to call or cross examine at a later jury trial.

Responding to Grand Jury Document Requests

In a busy judicial district, grand jury subpoenas for documents are issued and served on businesses daily. To some businesses (*e.g.,* banks, the telephone company, investment firms) the receipt of a grand jury subpoena is routine and uneventful. Other businesses, however, rarely if ever are served with grand jury process and the receipt of a subpoena prompts much speculation as to its significance. Quite frequently, and particularly in the early part of an investigation, subpoenas are issued generously by the government in an effort to capture for the agents documentary evidence of relationships or transactions that would only have become known to the government after many witness interviews. These subpoenas, typically issued far in advance of expected witness appearances before the grand jury, are often broad in scope. As such, the fact that a company has received a grand jury subpoena is no indication by itself of a cause for concern. In fact, it is not unusual for an investigation to be opened before a grand jury only to later lose momentum and quietly die after voluminous records have been accumulated.

The grand jury subpoena will typically bear the name and telephone number of the prosecutor. It may also invite the voluntary production of documents to an agent, who will then also be identified on the subpoena. Appended to the subpoena may be a schedule of documents to be produced. Prosecutors and agents may request on the face of the subpoena, or through an accompanying letter, that subpoena recipients not disclose the subpoenas to third persons. Compliance with such requests is usually voluntary, as only in rare cases (where a statue or court order permits it) may a prosecutor legally command that recipients not disclose the existence of a subpoena to others. Nonetheless, some entities – such as banks – are actually prohibited by law from disclosing their receipt of a subpoena concerning a customer even without a request by the government to keep the subpoena confidential. While best practice for a company is not to disclose to third parties the receipt of a subpoena, disclosure is usually not illegal and will not ordinarily be viewed by the government as amounting to an obstruction of justice – the investigation has become, through the issuance of the subpoena, *"overt"* and with that the government assumes the risk that the investigation will be become publically known to targets of the investigation or even to the general public. Still, prosecutors routinely ask witnesses who appear before them to identify to whom the witness disclosed the existence of a subpoena or with whom the witness spoke prior to appearing. Such questioning can become uncomfortable for the witness, particularly when the witness has discussed the subpoena and the investigation with persons who may be under active investigation.

Prosecutors are well-accustomed to receiving, after their issuance of a subpoena to a business, a call from the company served, or its counsel, to inquire about the investigation. Typically, while courteous and professional, prosecutors will say very little about who or what they are investigating. Nonetheless, receipt of a subpoena by a company or person that was expecting eventually to be contacted by law enforcement provides a convenient *entrée* for counsel to attempt to establish a dialogue with the government and to inquire as to whether the company or its managers are considered subjects or targets of the investigation. If the receipt by a business of a grand jury subpoena is not a matter of routine, the company is well-advised to consult immediately with counsel. Careful review of the terms and scope of the subpoena may well reveal to the experienced white-collar practitioner items of interest regarding the prosecutor's perception of the company or one or more of its executives.

Purposeful destruction of responsive documents upon receiving a subpoena is a crime. The deliberate destruction of relevant documents upon learning that a grand jury is investigating a matter – whether or not a subpoena has been served on that person – is also a crime. Disclosing the existence of a grand jury subpoena, with the hope and ultimate purpose that the recipient of the news will conceal or destroy evidence, is a crime. Withholding responsive documents at the time of the return of the records to the grand jury, when designed to impede the functions of the grand jury, is a crime. Talking to a witness who has been or is expected to be subpoenaed to appear before a grand jury and suggesting lines of defense or testimony may, depending on the circumstances, be considered witness tampering and is a crime. When any of the above occurs, prosecutors get very excited. Often an effort at obstruction will serve as powerful evidence that the actor knows he or she is guilty, and can be used as direct proof of the defendant's guilt in the trial of the underlying *substantive* offense (for example, a defendant's attempt falsely to suggest to a witness a timeline of events that might support an alibi defense to the crime of robbery can be introduced before the jury and argued as direct proof that the defendant committed the robbery). At other times, efforts to obstruct an investigation may prompt the bringing of criminal charges in circumstances where substantive charges would not otherwise have been pursued.

Accordingly, the process by which documents are gathered and produced by a business to the grand jury should be a matter of great care and thought. Some recommended practices:

* Issue a "*litigation hold*" communication at the first suggestion that the company may be receiving any subpoena – civil, criminal or regulatory – advising persons having documents or access to electronic records that the company has a duty to preserve all records relating to a particular controversy or event. If not done before receipt of a subpoena, work on such a preservation letter, and all other reasonable steps to preserve evidence, must commence.

* Select one person to coordinate the gathering of documents. That person should be someone who is uninvolved in the transaction under scrutiny. The business should feel comfortable that the person selected will be able to withstand the sometimes-stressful grand jury appearance that might follow.

* Suspend the normal corporate document retention (*i.e., routine destruction*) program. The fact that responsive documents are destroyed after receipt of a subpoena will be a matter of huge concern to the government, whether the destruction was the function of routine internal housekeeping processes or not.

* Halt entirely the recycling (and functional erasure) of *back up* tapes of company servers.

* Obtain control of all responsive documents and data as soon as practicable. If the company has been given three weeks to produce documents, gather the records within two. Be mindful of the need to review e-mails and other electronically-stored data for the existence of legal privilege. The company may also need to have conversations with its lawyers about whether certain documents are in fact responsive. Better practice, when in doubt, is to produce.

* Do not unnecessarily publish the fact that the company has received a subpoena. Do not make and circulate copies of the subpoena. Be discrete.

* Ensure that the designated *"document custodian"* – the person who may be called upon to appear before the grand jury – has kept accurate and detailed records of what documents were looked for, where, and from whom. The custodian should as well document the source and location of responsive documents.

* Consult counsel as appropriate regarding employee privacy rights and possible immunity issues. While receipt of a corporate subpoena does not mean that, simply because an officer or employee has personal documents at his or her work area, the documents are possessed by the company and must be produced. Conversely, the fact that an employee has business records or data at home or on personal computers does not make the records immune from production.

* Do not rely on individual employees to gather responsive records from their work areas, or emails and files from their computers. While the employee might take offense at having his or her files separately reviewed by others, or his or her laptop or computer being searched, the negative effect on employee morale is far outweighed by the negative consequences of an incomplete disclosure.

* When in doubt, talk to an attorney.

Witness Appearances

As mentioned, there is no judge in attendance during grand jury sessions. And most often the grand jury sits in a room that does not resemble a courtroom at all. A witness called before it will see the grand jury room occupied only by the witness, the prosecutor, a court reporter responsible for preparing a verbatim transcript of any testimony given, and the grand jurors. The grand jury foreperson will administer an oath. The prosecutor will lead the questioning, but at times grand jurors may ask questions too. While the fact that there is neither judge nor counsel present to watch the work of the prosecutor, instances of abuses by the prosecutor – abuses in the questioning of witnesses or abuses of the grand jury process itself – are rare.

The most important obligation of a witness is to tell the truth. The witness' choices are to: (a) invoke the Fifth Amendment and decline to testify on that basis or (b) tell the truth and the entire truth. There is never an option to lie, make partial disclosures or otherwise deceive the grand jury. The consequences of doing so once uncovered (and such things usually are) will ordinarily be devastating. Once the decision is made to talk, one must talk honestly, and without equivocation.

Much of the discussion in Chapter III pertaining to the informal law enforcement interview and the terms under which a witness will agree to provide information to the government applies here. We repeat here some of the material there covered, but in much abbreviated form:

If in doubt as to the witness' *status*, the recipient of a grand jury subpoena should, with the assistance of conflict-free counsel, set out to ascertain the government's characterization of the witness as a *"subject," "target"* or mere *"witness"* in the investigation. A careful assessment of the matter under investigation must be had, and a clear understanding of the client's role in the events at issue obtained, so that counsel can appropriately determine whether it is prudent or advisable for the witness to invoke his or her Fifth Amendment right not to testify.

If it appears that the witness is in fact a *subject* or may ultimately become a *target* of the investigation, counsel may initiate a dialogue with the government regarding some form of immunity protection. A witness cannot make a blanket Fifth Amendment assertion of rights and refuse to appear entirely. *"Taking the Fifth"* must be done on a question-by-question basis. And while, as previously noted, counsel may not be present in the grand jury to help the witness, the witness has the absolute right to consult with his or her counsel before answering a question. Accordingly, absent abuse of the procedure by a witness, the prosecutor must allow the witness to leave the grand jury room to consult with counsel, sometimes on a question-by-question basis. If the Fifth Amendment right is invoked, the witness will usually read a short statement from a script drafted by counsel for that purpose. The witness may invoke the

Fifth Amendment right as to some areas of questioning and yet answer other questions freely.

There may be times where counsel will not be satisfied with a prosecutor's letter agreement bestowing on the witness use and derivative use immunity. Remember from our discussion in Chapter III that a prosecutor in one judicial district cannot necessarily bind a prosecutor in another as to immunity issues. There are different forms of agreements used by different federal prosecution offices. Some offices litter their agreements with numerous conditions the non-compliance of any of which may serve, at the prosecutor's complete discretion, to void the agreement and the protections that were extended to the witness. Accordingly, there are times where prudent counsel will, in order to eliminate such limitations, ask that the prosecutor obtain *"statutory"* court-ordered immunity. That form of immunity – while also only *"use and derivative use"* immunity – is granted without conditions that the local prosecutors' office might ordinarily superimpose on it. The order is also effective nationwide, giving the witness protection against use and derivative uses by any federal prosecution office in the United States.

At other times a witness will refuse to testify after a prosecutor has offered immunity protection not because of the form of the agreement but because the witness simply does not want to testify against a friend or colleague or family member. Should the prosecutor wish to force the issue, the government must get an order conferring upon the witness statutory use immunity. If after being granted statutory immunity a witness continues to refuse to testify, the witness will usually be brought before the court that ordered the immunity, where the witness will be further ordered to testify (the grant of statutory immunity eliminates the witness' objection to being required to provide information that might be incriminating, and thus can then be forced to testify over his or her *constitutional* objection). Should the witness continue to refuse to testify, he or she may be held in contempt of court and sanctioned – including through continuing incarceration – until the witness relents and testifies.

Chapter 5

⸺◆⸻

Keeping an Eye on the End Game:
Attaining Acceptable Results

We warned above of the danger of projecting or *telescoping* ahead negatively to all of the consequences that might flow from the government's initiation of an investigation or its commencement of a regulatory enforcement action. That admonition applies particularly as necessary to the avoidance and management of potential crisis points that may surface in the days and weeks immediately after an investigation has revealed itself. Government investigations may take many months, even years, to come to conclusion. An initial show of force by the government at the outset of a matter – such as through the media-attention-grabbing execution of a search warrant or a blitz of rapid succession "*drop in*" interviews of managers and employees – will invariably be followed by periods of relative calm and time for reflection. Occasionally, some investigations go away after a while without much explanation by the government. The initial investigative hypothesis of the existence of some larger corporate plot might be determined to be unfounded or might prove too difficult to develop to the point of establishing the guilt of any individual at trial. Uneducated and panicky speculation by management of what might lie months or even years ahead risks distracting the company from paying careful attention to the important tasks immediately at hand during those critical early days of the investigation.

Yet it would be equally dangerous entirely to lose sight of the range of possible bad outcomes ahead. Even if likely to occur well into the future, they will often have a real-time impact on the company's business when they eventually occur – these consequences need to be planned for and factored into current decision-making. The possibility that the government may ultimately insist on the company's entering into a plea agreement may profoundly affect the wisdom of pursuing current investment and business opportunities. An eventual *"corporate plea"* may also result in a devastating government procurement debarment or the company's exclusion from federal program payments – eventualities that require the early development of strategies involving at times multiple government agencies to prevent their occurrence. Investors or the Board of Directors may ultimately demand changes at the top, and thus the Board's quiet attention to succession planning may be appropriate. The business might also be wise to assess the wisdom of suspending specific senior, mid- and lower-level employees pending the results of the government's work. Terminations might need to be considered. Resolution of these issues will all be complicated by the often complete uncertainty as to who is or may later become a *"subject"* or *"target"* of the investigation and of the government's timetable towards completion of its work.

Due to the importance to the business of keeping an eye on the ultimate *"end game"* scenarios, company counsel is likely to recommend that two things happen at the very outset of an investigation:

First, there will rarely be a time where a company determines not to communicate to the government an early and unequivocal pledge of full cooperation. There is likely to be a very protracted dialogue with the government during the investigation, not only about final outcomes but of collateral consequences of the investigation occurring along the way, and a constructive tone needs to be set straight away.

Second – and this often happens simultaneously – counsel needs to begin to have a candid conversation with the investigators as to what the government is trying to establish through its investigation. For obvious reasons, an early appreciation of the direction and scope of a government investigation – and particularly of the government's perception of "*how high up*" in the organization misconduct may have occurred – is critical.

Sometimes the government is very transparent about what it is investigating. Many other times, however, authorities will play their cards very close to the vest. Far too often meaningful conversation with the government about its case comes only towards the end of an investigation, and then only after the government has determined that it is ready to proceed against the company or senior executives. The challenge is for the company to understand as much as it can about possible outcomes as early as it can.

This Chapter focuses, then, on the "*end game.*" The government is not likely just to go away. What are the outcomes the government has set out to achieve? And after the investigation draws to a conclusion, what might the government eventually do to the company? To its managers and employees? Does the government have institutional pressures to achieve certain results? What options does the company have to guide the matter to a conclusion that everyone can live with?

A Hypothetical -- The *"Corporate Plea"*

Consider the following scenario:

The last 20 months of government scrutiny of the Genetics Division has been full of twists and turns -- and it has been positively draining. What initially looked like an investigation focusing only on a handful of communications between some west coast "ops" managers and a couple of billing clerks about very technical billing protocols has spawned into a wide-ranging inquiry into corruption and certain aggressive revenue recognition practices seemingly orchestrated by the founder of Real Genetics, Inc. (now a member of your Board of Directors and the Audit Committee). To compound matters, not only had some documents gone missing very early on in the investigation but there were suggestions that electronic data had been purged or altered, contributing to another line of government investigation focusing on several senior finance officers at not just the Division level but at corporate headquarters.

Deep management paralysis has set in. Expansion plans into new markets were shelved long ago. And while there had been appetite by the Board to explore a merger opportunity that had been recently presented, no one had any insight as to what the results of the government's investigation were going to be, stalling discussion of the proposal. The Board was becoming increasingly frustrated and its Chairman, who had very loudly and often protested the company's innocence, was beginning to agitate internally that the company simply needed to get this thing behind it, no matter the cost. While your outside counsel had met with the government several months ago, she had come back with only unsatisfactory assurances from the lead prosecutor that a full discussion of the case would come when the time was ripe. That time never seemed to come.

Yesterday your legal team had another meeting with the prosecutors handling the investigation. This time there had been a reasonable expectation that a real dialogue with the government might finally begin. Counsel's pre-meeting request that the prosecutors' supervisor attend had been accepted by the government without hesitation. In fact, counsel was told that the US Attorney herself would be at the meeting, prompting optimism that they were finally seeing the light at the end of the tunnel. The marching orders to counsel were clear: do whatever it might take to prompt a discussion towards a concrete "corporate" resolution of the matter, to include at least suggesting the potential of the company's agreeing to a very substantial fine. Your Chairman had insisted, however, that a resolution could not involve a formal admission of guilt by the company. Although the government was not to be told of the amount of money the company might pay, internal discussions centered on an estimate, based on public reports of fines imposed in similar cases, that the company might have to pay between $50 and $100 million to obtain peace.

At this morning's executive management meeting, counsel reported only bad news. The government apparently had started the discussion by expressing confidence that it had proof of a multi-year Medicare fraud scheme involving the manipulation by the Genetics Division of numerous billing procedure codes, and by further pronouncing that it would be willing to resolve the case against the company only if the company took a corporate plea to at least one felony count. Although initially taken aback, your legal team countered that a disposition involving a non-prosecution agreement and the payment of a stipulated penalty, or the entry of a "deferred prosecution agreement," would equally vindicate the government's interests while avoiding the several very real negative consequences that the entry of a guilty plea would bring to the company and its investors. Counsel forecast that a guilty plea would unquestionably bring with it the company's exclusion from participation in the Medicare program and that the market reaction to that development would be devastating. Business lines would have to abandoned and employees would be laid off. The lead prosecutor seemed to brush that off, adding without comment that any disposition would involve fines and penalties exceeding $300 million. When counsel argued that that amount was grossly disproportionate to any actual losses the government might ever be able to prove, the lead prosecutor curiously cited the disappearance of critical evidence in apparent obstruction of the investigation and the involvement of high level corporate executives in the scheme. In fact, one junior member of the prosecution team offered that, in light of "management's" efforts to derail the investigation, and given that the founder of the Genetics Division was "at the center" of the scheme, the government might also insist on the appointment of a "corporate monitor" to oversee the company's compliance with the corporate integrity program the government would be insisting on as a term of any plea agreement. The US Attorney, quiet to that point, chimed in that Medicare fraud was one of the most important priorities of her Office, and that whatever other districts and even "Main Justice" had done to resolve similar cases was entirely irrelevant.

Your counsel, as had been directed by the Board, attempted to determine whether the government intended to charge individuals, and, if so, who. The conversation went cold at that point. Your attorney's effort to suggest that any large monetary settlement would have to be in exchange for finality and cessation of the matter as to both the company and any and all individuals who might otherwise be charged was met with a chuckle from the lead prosecutor. Added his boss, the US Attorney, "We won't bargain any man's liberty for dollars." When asked when the government might make charging decisions if the case could not be resolved, the prosecutors stated only that any formal charges were still a good number of months away.

Subject only to the (rarely occurring) disagreement by a federal grand jury, the government has virtually unfettered discretion in criminal cases to decide who will be charged, who will be spared, what charges will be brought, and when charges will be sought. It is almost always in the best interests of a business to have discussions about possible resolutions involving the company well before the government makes charging decisions. While it might take considerable coaxing to get the government to speak about its case, the government will not, as a rule, lie about its intentions during pre-charge discussions with counsel when they finally do occur. Those discussions also typically will reveal that the government has no desire whatever of seeing a company go out of business, employees laid off, or creditors, investors and vendors unnecessarily harmed. Because of this desire by the government to avoid causing innocent persons harm, there should always be room to argue factors in mitigation of harsh charging decisions. Still, because the government, from a programmatic standpoint, banks on the deterrent effect that corporate pleas and executive-level convictions and jail time sentencings will have on other businesses operating in the defendant's industry, the government may remain resolved to lay a heavy blow on a business that has profited from wrongdoing, despite even an early admission of responsibility and promptly initiated remediation.

All of this underscores the critical importance the internal investigation (addressed in Chapter I) will play in informing counsel and management as early as possible as to the likely strength of the government's evidence, the pervasiveness of any misconduct, the likelihood that individual charges might be brought against executives, and the probable timing of any government charging decisions. Such an investigation will also usually serve to put the company in the best position to fully and proactively cooperate with the government in its investigation as well as to inform early remedial actions by the company. While pre-charge discussions will always involve an exchange about the facts and the magnitude of harms supposedly caused, a company's genuine cooperation with the government in its investigation coupled with very early steps to remedy past wrongs may be the most important talking points your counsel will have when speaking to the government about dispositions. A company's early decision to accept responsibility, cooperate and to implement or tighten existing compliance protocols (the subject of Chapter VI below) can have a dramatically positive impact on the outcome of even the bleakest of cases.

When contemplating end-game strategies, management may find itself addressing a number of interesting legal and procedural issues:

Why would the government ever expect *the company* itself to plead guilty? If any criminal violations occurred, they were the result of egregious misconduct by employees whose actions were not only unauthorized but in violation of clear company policy. How did the company itself commit a crime?

Just from a fairness standpoint, should not the government go after the persons who committed these offenses? A *corporate* guilty plea is going to have all sorts of negative consequences to the company and to innocent constituents of the business.

Most of the conduct the government has looked at involved a corporate predecessor that does not even exist today. Why should the company bear the brunt for another company's misconduct?

The company pays a lot of money to lobbyists. Is it ever appropriate to ask a legislator to demand a review in Washington of the decisions being made by the local prosecution team?

If the company must plead guilty to a felony, what will be the company's exposure? What are the maximum sanctions that might be imposed? Can the company get the court involved early on to ensure that a fair resolution is achieved?

The company has at every turn cooperated with the government and provided information that the grand jury would have taken years to develop. Doesn't the company get credit for that? What about all the effort it put into fine tuning its compliance program after the investigation started?

Even if the company resolves its case with the government, there is no guarantee that individual employees – if they are charged too – will go away quietly. There may be continued media attention to this whole sordid affair for years to come. Why is the government so insistent that they will not do a *"global resolution,"* sparing individuals from prosecution?

If charged, what do employees face, in terms of sentencing, if found guilty? What kind of *plea deals* might the government be offering them? Does the company have any say in the matter of what happens to its employees?

Avoiding the Worst Case -- Alternatives to the Corporate Criminal Conviction

The government's investigation and prosecution of business crimes presents unique considerations requiring the government's exercise of greatly informed and deliberate judgment. Companies always operate at risk that employees will engage in misconduct that will subject the business to civil lawsuits or regulatory sanctions. But should not criminal prosecution of a business be reserved for use only in the most egregious cases, and in cases where there is significant senior level involvement in the crimes? In considering whether to bring criminal charges, however, the government's focus is not necessarily going to be driven by a consideration of the appropriate measure of punishment that will be exacted upon the company in light of the business' relative culpability as a wrong-doer. The government usually calculates that, when bringing charges directly against a business, an entire industry segment will be deterred from engaging in similar illegal business practices. By the same token, the government will also readily recognize that this so-called "*deterrence*" objective ought not ordinarily be achieved at the expense of entirely innocent company stakeholders in the business – owners, employees, suppliers, even consumers – who did not in any way profit from misdeeds that are often committed by a relative handful of employees.

Absent such harm to innocent third parties, however, the argument alone that there is unfairness in charging a corporation or other entity with the commission of a crime absent widespread misconduct within the company or absent some official, high level endorsement of the criminal acts will rarely carry the day with a prosecution team. To the surprise of many clients, the law permits a company to be charged even if its management has been entirely oblivious to wrongdoing at lower levels. The legal criminal exposure companies bear for the misdeeds of even remote, rogue employees thus deserves some treatment below before we get to a broader discussion of the factors that typically influence the government's discretion to charge not only individual offenders, but the business itself, with the commission of criminal offenses.

A Side Note on Corporate Criminal Liability

It has long been legally established that a company – whether a corporation, partnership or other entity form of business – is itself criminally responsible for the crimes of its individual employees, at whatever level, if (a) the employee was acting within the scope of his or her assigned duties and (b) the misdeeds were motivated at least in part by a desire to benefit the company. A corollary doctrine applies criminal exposure to a company even for the prior wayward acts of an entirely separate business that is eventually acquired and merged into the company. The corporate successor to a bad company remains responsible for pre-acquisition misdeeds. We work through both scenarios immediately below.

Consider, first, the case of the employee that deliberately sets out illegally to bill the government for services never actually performed, in violation of clear company policy that prohibits dishonest billings, all done by the employee in a manner to avoid detection by his employer, the company, and motivated only by a desire by the employee to get a better cash bonus at the end of the year. Did the employee act outside the scope of employment thus absolving the company from liability? After all, the misconduct violated clear policy and was never condoned by management. The law says, "*No*," this conduct, even if criminal, was within the scope of the employment. If the employee, as part of his or her duties, was expected to bill the government for services, he or she acted within the scope of assigned responsibilities when submitting claims for payment, no matter their falsity and no matter the deviation from company policy. Well, what about the required motivation to benefit the company? Here the employee was driven to cheat so that he could profit personally. The employee was never thinking, goes the argument, that what he was doing was truly in the best interests of the company, done to benefit the business. Applying the legal doctrine of *repondeat superior,* however, a federal court will hold the company criminally responsible if at least one objective of the activity was to do something that would even incidentally benefit the company – in this case, one intended result was to increase, albeit fraudulently, corporate revenues so as ultimately to justify a higher year-end bonus. Corporate criminal liability attaches.

To the board of directors of the company, it will seem an unfair government overreach to charge the company for this activity – this was a rogue employee, after all, and the media attention that may follow the corporate criminal charge may scare away customers, unfairly advantage competitors, upset potential investors and creditors and cast a pall over the integrity of the entire enterprise and its employees. But a government decision to prosecute a company may result in immediate restitution and other forms of corporate remediation. More importantly, it might deter others in the company from cheating. It may send a wide message across the business community that the government stands ready to prosecute aggressively all forms of business dishonesty, spurring companies to double down on their investment in compliance protocols designed to prevent and detect fraud.

Consider, second, the acquisition by a business of a company that represents a venture into an entirely new line of business – and maybe even into an entirely new geographic market – and with it a new set of laws, rules, regulations and regulators. Very generally speaking (and there are legal and transactional strategies that can be used to avoid this result), the acquiring business is going to inherit even entirely hidden enforcement problems of the acquired company. A contrary result would encourage businesses to play a corporate shell game to avoid the consequences of criminal behavior. To the entirely innocent acquirer, however, this outcome will seem unfair. Plainly, equities will lie with the acquiring company when attempting to negotiate a corporate *pass* from the government for criminal responsibility based on the acts of a predecessor, but the exposure will not be entirely avoidable (underscoring, of course, the need for thorough pre-acquisition due diligence).

We outline in the following pages the several unique factors the government typically takes into account when deciding whether or not to charge a company directly for the criminal conduct of employees and corporate predecessors, as well as some special procedural options the government some-times uses to dispose of these cases so as to prevent inequities and potential harm to innocent third parties. We also address the range of charging and sentencing outcomes generally facing individual wrongdoers within a com-pany, whether or not a company is also to be charged. However, in order adequately to frame discussion of these topics, some preliminary treatment of the rules and protocols relating generally to charging and sentencing processes is necessary

A Little Bit of History – On Sentencing and Charging Decisions

Once upon a time – but not so very long ago – the courts had maximum discretion to sentence an offender anywhere within a range of no jail time (or no fine) to the statutory *maximum* term of imprisonment or fine. By way of example, under prior federal sentencing protocols, if an offender was charged and found guilty of two offenses, one carrying a potential maximum sentence of five years and the other carrying a maximum term of 20 years, the courts had a host of options. The judge could "*throw the book*" at the defendant by requiring the defendant to serve the maximum term of imprisonment on each count and by "*stacking*" the sentence – to make them run "*consecutive*" to each other -- resulting in a 25-year jail term. Or the judge could alternatively sentence the defendant to five years on each count, and order the sentences to be run "*concurrent*" to each other, so that the defendant only had to serve a total five-year term of imprisonment. Or the judge could order that no jail time be served on either count, and impose only a modest fine and a term of non-supervised probation, during which the defendant would be required only not to commit new offenses. The courts under the former sentencing protocols could choose among an almost infinite combination of jail time, probationary terms and financial consequences. Sentences were also largely non-reviewable by the appellate courts, absent some legal error in the process.

This system resulted in sentencing proceedings before the courts that were wide-open affairs. On what was truly the day of reckoning, a defendant could summon his pastor, spouse, elementary school teacher, rabbi, employer, *etc.* to come to court to try to convince the sentencing judge that a prison term or other harsh sentence would serve little if any purpose at all, or would irreparably ruin the accused's life or harm third persons who were reliant on the freedom and continued productivity of the offender. Victims for their part also had a say, and courts could mete out justice driven by the individual predilections and judgments of the assigned judge as to the value of imprisonment and other harsh sentencing conditions in achieving the penologic objectives of deterrence, incapacitation, punishment and rehabilitation.

That prior sentencing regimen – one that provided individual courts full opportunity for *Solomonic*, majestic exercises of individual mercy (and merciless punishment, too) – began to give way 30-plus years ago to the criticism that, when viewed across the entirety of the U.S. judicial system, sentencing had become a wildly inconsistent process. A defendant sentenced by a lenient judge could walk out of court a free man while an identically-situated defendant in another part of the country (or even in another part of the courthouse), charged with the very same crime but sentenced before a harsh sentencing judge, could face many years of imprisonment.

Congress, in 1984, in a mood not only to eliminate the inconsistent treatment of defendants but to reign in what many policy-makers perceived as soft-on-crime sentencing judges, established the U.S. Sentencing Commission, and charged it with promulgating federal *Sentencing Guidelines* that would narrow dramatically the discretion with which courts could impose stricter or more lenient sentences. Congress also, as to a number of offenses (predominantly narcotics and firearms offenses), established harsh minimum sentences as to which all offenders had to be sentenced, thereby removing any judicial discretion to sentence a defendant to anything less than the statutory "*mandatory minimum.*" Congress at the same time abolished entirely "*parole,*" a tool that could be employed by the U.S. Parole Commission to obtain the early release of individuals viewed as receiving overly harsh sentences. Finally, Congress also in 1984 promulgated a "*truth-in-sentencing*" scheme requiring defendants sentenced to a term of imprisonment to serve 85 percent or more of their prison time. Abolished were the days where good behavior might result in an offender's release after service, say, of one-third or less of a sentence.

Sentencing in the federal courts thereafter became largely a mathematical affair and, by most accounts, a much harsher and less forgiving system. The U.S. Sentencing Commission in 1987 rolled out a complex categorization scheme – based on formula values assigned in accordance with the Commission's perception of the relative gravity of offenses and the characteristics of an offender – that the courts were *required* to apply when sentencing individuals. The Commission mandated judges to sentence persons only within certain very narrow ranges based on objective factors that the Commission set with mathematical precision. For example, a mail fraud offense bearing a five-year maximum term was categorized by the Commission as having a certain "*base offense level*" – again, using a point system that was based on the Sentencing Commission's impression of the relative severity of mail fraud as a species of crime – which sentencing base offense level could be increased upwards by the addition of points for aggravating factors, such as the extent of victim financial losses, the sophistication of the offense, the use of special skill in its commission, the individual's assumption of a leadership role in a scheme, and the prior criminal history of the defendant. A limited amount of points could likewise be reduced from the *Guidelines* calculation based on mitigating factors identified in the *Guidelines*, such as offender's early acceptance of responsibility, minimal role in the offense or other unique mitigating factors specifically identified in the *Guidelines*.

In our hypothetical mail fraud offense, the final score might be determined by the court to be a "*Level 19, Criminal History Factor II.*" That would leave the court to consult with the *Guidelines* "*Sentencing Table,*" revealing that the court had only the discretion to sentence the defendant before it within a range of 33 and 41 months. Sentencing within that final *Guideline* range was mandatory. Absent unusual factors outlined specifically in the *Guidelines*, a court could not "*depart*" upwards or downwards from the range without a specific finding being made justifying the departure based on extraordinary circumstances. To make sure that individual judges did not thwart the application of the *Guidelines*, every determination by the sentencing court (base offense level, role in the offense, aggravating and mitigating factors, departures, *etc.*) became appealable by either the defendant or the government. If the application of a disputed sentencing factor was unsupported by the record created at the time of sentencing, the matter was required to be reversed and sent back for resentencing.

To make matters worse for persons charged with business crimes – usually involving fraud charges – the *Guidelines'* focus on "*loss amount*" as the most critical sentencing factor resulted in required sentencings of white collar defendants within ranges of imprisonment rarely previously imposed by the courts in fraud cases.

As a result of these changes, contested sentencing hearings for persons convicted of business crimes often devolved into very intense debates between the prosecutor and defense counsel regarding loss amounts, a defendant's role in the offense, his or her use of special skill or sophisticated means in the commission of the crime, and the application of other aggravating and mitigating factors. Gone entirely were the days where sentencings were dominated by pleas of mercy, exhortations to impose harsh punishment based on the impacts on individual victims, and attempts to demonstrate the otherwise general good character and upbringing of a defendant.

Compounding all this – and very important to our current discussion – was the fact that *prosecutors* became far less able to exercise discretion as to which charges to bring. The opportunity to engage in liberal "*charge bargaining*" with prosecutors so as to reduce a defendant's maximum sentencing exposure was significantly limited -- not necessarily by the *Guidelines* themselves, but by government policy choice.

Prosecutors historically have had unreviewable discretion to decide what charges the government would charge a defendant. This discretion was quickly seen by the policy-makers who urged the promulgation of the *Guidelines* scheme to be a significant *weak link* in the then-newly-promulgated "*determinate sentencing*" scheme. Prosecutors retained the power to diminish an expected harsh sentence in any case by offering a defendant a plea to a single offense that carried a sentencing maximum (say, a five-year *cap*) that was well below the expected *Guideline* result that would obtain under the *Sentencing*

Table had a more serious offense (or series of offenses) been charged. Or the prosecutor could choose between types of offenses to achieve a lower Base Offense Level starting point. As a result, a defendant could through pre-indictment charge-bargaining with the government achieve a markedly different outcome depending upon which individual prosecutor in which of the 94-federal judicial districts a matter was brought.

Congress did not, however, attempt to limit a prosecutor's discretion as to whether any offense should be charged at all, or as to the selection of offenses that would be charged where a choice might exist. This congressional inaction reflected the judgment of Congress that it is the government, ultimately, that must be the sole arbitrator of whether it has accumulated evidence sufficient to support a conviction as to any individual offense. Every offense requires proof beyond a reasonable doubt of each and every unique *element* of the crime. Depending on the facts, not every offense potentially applicable to a particular scheme will be readily provable. Oftentimes an individual element of a specific crime will present a unique evidentiary challenge not existing as to the evidence available to establish a substantially-related offense. Prosecutors needed to be able to make those calls.

In order to eliminate sentencing disparities between like situated defendants caused by the exercise of prosecutorial charging discretion, the US Department of Justice today mandates that its prosecutors charge the "*most serious, readily provable offense*" available to be charged. Generally speaking, a prosecutor who opts to charge a "*less serious*" offense (severity being measured by the *Guidelines*) must justify the decision to do so and get supervisory approvals. While enforced only internally within the Department of Justice, any business or manager facing a criminal investigation must be aware that prosecutors may well find themselves telling defense counsel that, by internal Department policy, they have no choice but to seek the grand jury's return of charges to offenses requiring significant jail time under the *Guidelines*.

Over the last 30 years the pendulum has swung back and forth as to the amount of discretion recognized to reside in our courts and prosecutors to affect *Sentencing Guidelines* results. The Supreme Court a full 20 years after the passage of the Sentencing Reform Act in 1984 held that the *Guidelines* must be considered literally to be in the nature of *guidelines*, and thus *advisory*, and not, as had been understood, a form of inflexible, legislatively-mandated limitation on the power of the courts to sentence individuals anywhere within the very broad statutory ranges set by the statute creating the offense (*e.g.*, within 0-5 years for many offenses, or within 0-20 years for other more serious crimes). And the extent to which prosecutors have been able to exercise discretion in individual cases to achieve just results has varied from administration to administration. However, the above description of the federal sentencing scheme largely holds today – judges and prosecutors talk and analyze sentencing considerations in *Guidelines* language. Despite their advisory nature, the courts are still required to respect and largely honor the *Guidelines*. Most sentences today continue to fall within the ranges set out in the *Guidelines Sentencing Table* and decisions made by sentencing courts remain appealable. Most importantly, prosecutors accept the concept as well that the determinate sentencing system within which they work requires their sacrifice of the ability to exercise discretion in making charging decisions based only on perceived sentencing outcomes.

Charging the Corporate Defendant – Special Considerations, Deferred Prosecution and Non-Prosecution Agreements

The U.S. Department of Justice has published extremely useful guidelines intended to guide prosecutors throughout the country as to the factors relevant in making the decision whether or not to charge a business organization for offenses committed by its employees. In these internal "*DOJ*" communications prosecutors are given significant charging flexibility when it comes to charging *businesses* – notwithstanding the fairly rigid limits on charging discretion relating to *individuals*. Typically, a prosecutor investigating an individual has two principal choices: to charge or not to charge. As most immediately discussed above, once a decision to charge an individual has been made the prosecutor must proceed with the most serious of the available charges which the government has confidence it can establish at trial beyond a reasonable doubt.

The Department of Justice, however, has with respect to business organizations given prosecutors two additional charging options – the *"non-prosecution agreement"* (*"NPA"*) and the *"deferred prosecution agreement"* (*"DPA"*).

Under a non-prosecution agreement, a company can enter into an agreement with the government that promises that no charges will be brought against the company within a specified period of time (typically somewhere between two and five years) provided certain conditions are met. All non-prosecution agreements will require the company not to commit additional offenses during its term. But an *NPA* will also typically contain many more provisions covering a lot of additional subjects, all determined entirely at the discretion of the prosecution team. The government might, for example, in the *NPA* demand payment of an agreed-to civil money penalty or victim restitution amount; it may insist that the company adopt a rigorous internal compliance program and report to the government instances in which the company's Code of Conduct has been violated; it may require the promulgation of policies and procedures relating to particular business practices; it may insist that the company agree to the appointment of and payment for the costs of the installation of an outside "corporate monitor," having the power to examine the books and records of the company, to interview witnesses and to report back the government any post-*NPA* missteps or transgressions; and it will usually require an agreement to a negotiated statement of facts relating to the offenses under investigation. Still, a non-prosecution agreement will largely not interfere with the manner in which the business continues its operations, require that certain employees be terminated or insist that identified lines of business be abandoned. Most importantly, a company's entry into an *NPA* means it has not been charged or convicted of any offenses and that the government's investigation – as to the company, at least – is over.

A violation of a non-prosecution agreement can, in the government's discretion, result in criminal charges being filed related to the activity that had been the subject of the government's initial investigation leading to the entry of the *NPA*, as well as based upon any additional violations discovered after the execution of the *NPA*. Upon conclusion of the term of the *NPA*, the company is relieved of any further obligations and the government is held to its commitment not to charge the company for any offenses arising out of the circumstances that led to the execution of the *NPA*.

A deferred prosecution agreement is very similar, in terms of the flexibility afforded to the government to impose such conditions as the establishment of compliance and reporting protocols, civil monetary penalties, *etc*. The difference, however, is that a deferred prosecution agreement involves the public filing with the court of a formal written criminal charge – in the form of an agreed upon *"Information"* – but accompanied by a commitment by the government, in a written agreement, that the prosecutors will *defer* prosecution of the crimes charged pending the company's satisfactory compliance with the terms of the *DPA*. That means that a court will be involved in supervising enforcement of the terms of the agreement. Like the non-prosecution agreement, a deferred prosecution agreement will typically require a company to agree in writing to a detailed set of facts that the government can use against the business if the *DPA* falls apart. Accordingly, should a violation of the deferred prosecution agreement occur the government need do no further work to investigate the case – prosecution of the then-pending charges is no longer deferred, but is activated and moves forward with the company having little if any possibility of interposing a defense to the charges. If the terms of the *DPA* have been satisfied, the government is obligated to dismiss the pending charges with no prospect of later resurrecting them.

In addressing the unique availability to prosecutors of *NPA*s and *DPA*s to dispose of cases against business entities, the Department of Justice transparently recognizes that the charging of companies is wrought with the possibility of unintended collateral consequences to the company, employees, and other innocent business constituents having an interest in the continued viability of an enterprise. Indeed, the Department has gone so far as to make clear that the availability of civil or regulatory penalties (as well as the availability of charges brought against company employees) may well sufficiently vindicate the government's interest in enforcing the rule of law as to serve as a substitute entirely to the bringing of formal criminal charges against a company.

None of this is to suggest, however, that the Department of Justice has signaled to its local prosecution teams across the United States that it is appropriate to go soft on corporate wrongdoers and to charge business entities only reluctantly and rarely. To the contrary, the prosecution of corporate crime has often been announced as one of the highest priorities of the Department of Justice. Criminal prosecution of business entities is seen as an important tool in enforcing the rule of law, securing the integrity of capital markets, protecting consumers and discouraging dishonest practices that adversely affect fair competition in the market place. The Department extolls to its prosecutors the need for *"[v]igorous enforcement of the criminal laws against corporate wrongdoers."* The Department exhorts that *"[i]ndicting corporations [themselves] for wrongdoing enables the government to be a force for positive change of corporate culture...."*

Practically every law enforcement program – federal or state, and those of regulatory agencies as well – operate largely on the proposition that the aggressive charging and punishment of business offenders will achieve important *"deterrent effects"* necessary to the general success of their enforcement efforts. Not every offender can be discovered and charged. There are insufficient law enforcement resources available to prosecute every business that violates the law. But the swift, high profile punishment of persons and companies that have the misfortune of falling within the crosshairs of an investigation is seen by the government as a powerful message to business associates, competitors, and executives within entire industry segments that the government can and will prosecute wrongdoers – and that those persons responsible for business crimes can and will be sent to jail.

The Department of Justice has devoted substantial resources to the prosecution of business crimes – the Department's Antitrust Division, Environmental & Natural Resources Division, and Tax Division have highly developed criminal enforcement programs; DOJs *"Main Justice"* Criminal Division in Washington D.C. has also at any given time literally hundreds of specialized Foreign Corrupt Practices Act, Medicare fraud and corruption investigations underway. All of these programs, and the economic crimes prosecution teams based in the 94 U.S. Attorney's Offices throughout the country, rely on this power of deterrence to keep businesses honest. The effectiveness of deterrence as a law enforcement tool depends upon the swift and certain punishment of crimes brought to the government's attention. There is no inherent pressure within the system for prosecutors and agents to be soft on business offenders. To the contrary.

The federal principles of prosecutions relating to business organizations suggest a number of factors that prosecutors are to take into account in exercising the "*thoughtful and pragmatic judgment [necessary] to achieve a fair and just outcome and promote respect for the law*" by business organizations. Most of the elements relevant to whether a prosecutor should decide to indict a company, rather than opting for the *DPA / NPA* middle road, or to a decision not to charge at all, are firmly grounded in common sense:

* * How pervasive within the organization was the misconduct?
* * How serious was the misconduct?
* * Is the company a repeat offender?
* * Were high level personnel involved?
* * Did the company voluntarily report the misconduct once detected?
* * Has it accepted responsibility and cooperated fully and promptly with the government
* * Did the company have a pre-existing compliance program?
* * Has it committed promptly to a course of remediation, provided restitution to victims, effected the termination of bad employees, or improved compliance protocols?

Accordingly, any business facing a significant criminal investigation needs to begin preparing itself very early on towards positioning itself to convince the government to consider the use of unique non-criminal dispositions, such as the employment of an *NPA* or *DPA*, as an alternative to the corporate plea. That means for most companies the early commencement of an internal investigation and a clear communication to the government of a willingness to share the results of its investigation. Prompt remediation, early self-reporting, termination of bad employees, enhancement of compliance protocols, effecting restitution to known victims, and other steps that demonstrate the business's genuine acceptance of responsibility can go tremendous lengths towards achieving a non-criminal disposition.

The company should also have made a detailed and sophisticated economic analysis of the potential impacts the compelled entry of a plea will have on the company, investors, its employees and the communities in which the company works. Remember that the government typically attempts to ameliorate negative consequences to innocent third parties, and nuanced modeling and financial calculations based on likely lost revenues -- as will occur when a plea triggers an automatic federal debarment or program exclusion consequence, or that may occur due to loss of competitive market position -- may be persuasive, particularly if the analysis suggests the possibility of employee layoffs or injury to companies in the businesses supply chain. And, if the company is not in a position financially to shoulder the sorts of mega fines that have been increasingly imposed on businesses (exceeding in some rare cases $1 billion, but easily exceeding $100 million in more routine prosecutions of large businesses), an *"ability to pay"* analysis should be completed. Bottom line, a company seriously at risk of being charged criminally should position itself to demonstrate an inability to pay a large fine without substantial negative impact on the company, to demonstrate the often-ruinous impact of a debarment or exclusion decision by a procurement authority, or to show likely resulting harms to innocent investors, employees and other third parties should formal charges be sought.

Charging the Corporate Executive and Mid-Level Manager

The strategic options available to a corporate executive or mid-level manager implicated in a corporate criminal scheme are considerably fewer.

The Department of Justice strongly admonishes its prosecutors that:

One of the most effective ways to combat corporate misconduct is by holding accountable all individuals who engage in wrongdoing.... Prosecutors should focus on wrongdoing by individuals from the very beginning of any investigation of corporate misconduct.... *Provable individual culpability should be pursued, particularly if it relates to high-level corporate officers, even in the face of an offer of a corporate guilty plea*

> *or some other disposition of the charges against the corporation, including*
> *a deferred prosecution or non-prosecution agreement, or a civil resolution.*

(Emphasis added). When combined with the fact addressed above that prosecutors are duty bound to prosecute against individuals the *"most serious, readily provable offense"* punishable under the *Sentencing Guidelines*, managers who become subjects or targets of an investigation of corporate misconduct face particular peril. Not only do the *Sentencing Guidelines* dictate jail time in fraud prosecutions involving significant losses, but the company will have, for the reasons outlined immediately above, a strong early motivation to provide to the government evidence of the individual's malfeasance.

Counsel representing an at-risk manager typically has few cards to play except to work to demonstrate to the government that his or her client had no personal involvement in advancing or profiting from the scheme. Other times the best course is to sit tight. In a not insignificant number of cases the government finds itself unable even after a lengthy investigation to proceed with confidence with charges against marginally-involved employees. In those circumstances, working too hard to convince the government not to indict can backfire. Accepting a seemingly benign government invitation to have one's client sit for a *"queen for a day"* debriefing to demonstrate to the government the employee's innocence may itself be fraught with danger, notwithstanding the immunity protection extended by the government. Under the enormous stress of such an interview, clients can easily manifest uncertainty or unnatural caution in responding to questions that can be mistaken by the government for dishonesty. It is understatement to say that nothing good ever comes from a prosecutor or agent believing that a subject of an investigation is not telling the truth. A bad proffer session may breathe new life into an investigation, encouraging a prosecutor to dig deeper and work harder. Significant focused discussion between a lawyer and his client must happen before risking such an encounter with prosecutors and agents.

While there will, then, in fact be times when the only prudent course available to the manager under investigation is to wait out an investigation and to steel oneself for the prospect of contesting charges at trial, there will always be huge motivations for an at-risk manager or employee to resolve his or her situation with the government. Absent an indemnification provision in corporate by laws covering the cost of the defense of any action brought against the employee arising out of his or her employment, an employee's self-financing of the defense of any significant investigation or criminal trial will be extremely burdensome. Regrettably, all too often these sorts of financial considerations will lead to discussions between lawyer and client regarding the employee's ability to provide the government with evidence and testimony necessary to help prosecute persons with greater complicity in the scheme. Unpleasant as is often the prospect of turning on former business associates and friends, the earlier a client gets to the government the greater the likelihood that the government will be prepared generously to reward cooperation.

Indeed, another more compelling motivation to abandon a defensive posture and to cooperate with the government exists. As noted above, the *Guidelines* suggest the imposition of often harsh and mathematically-derived sentencing outcomes – *unless* an unusual factor exists justifying a court to make a permitted *"downward departure."* One of the most readily available ways for a criminal defendant to receive a downward departure from an otherwise substantial *Sentencing Guidelines* disposition is through cooperation with the government. Under the *Guidelines*, to secure a downward departure based on cooperation the prosecution team has to affirmatively ask the court for the departure. A court cannot grant a *"cooperation"* downward departure on its own volition nor can a departure be granted on the motion of a defendant. Only the government may ask for a departure based on cooperation. Obviously, the government's ability to make an effective recommendation to obtain such a departure is an enormous weapon in a prosecutor's already well-stocked arsenal of investigative and enforcement tools.

The Letter of Apology

This will never happen.

There are certainly times that the government will *decline* to prosecute a matter entirely. While defense counsel may jokingly announce that he or she is working hard to obtain from the government the proverbial "*letter of apology*" for even commencing an investigation, the reality is that when declinations occur they most often happen silently, without fanfare or public announcement. The government has no obligation even to tell a subject or target of an investigation that, as an internal matter, the prosecutor has decided to suspend or abandon its investigation. Prosecutors are, nonetheless, as a rule responsible, courteous and civil, and will act responsibly in advising an otherwise anxious subject of an investigation that a matter has been concluded. More often than not, such communication is informally done between the government and a client's defense lawyer. But issue a letter of apology? Never.

The point here is that there will in fact be times when matters that appeared at one point on a certain path to indictment and eventual trial end unexpectedly and for reasons never fully communicated by the government. Sometimes this is the result of the advocacy of defense counsel in exposing weaknesses in the government's case. Other times, things just happen – witnesses become unavailable, government personnel having an interest in the matter are reassigned, initial investigative hypothesizes crumble under the weight of grand jury testimony. Obviously, the occurrence of this sort of outcome is never to be banked on.

Chapter 6

An Ounce of Prevention – The Maintenance of a Robust *"Culture of Compliance"*

There has been in the last 20 years increasing acceptance in the business community that the implementation of a company-wide *corporate compliance and integrity program* is an essential business risk management measure. A good compliance program can serve to reduce the risk of many different types of injury to a business, to include civil liability, losses due to fraud and theft, and sanctions flowing from regulatory infractions. It can also help avoid or reduce the much more dramatic harms that may flow from a company's becoming the subject of a criminal investigation and prosecution.

In the last five chapters, we outlined the parade of horribles that can be visited on a business whose employees engage in conduct that violate our criminal laws. We posit in this Chapter that investment in a genuinely-motivated compliance program is the *ounce of prevention* that every prudent business organization should take to avoid the often-devastating consequences – lost business, legal fees, tarnished reputations, company valuation losses, ruined careers and incalculable heartache, stress and business disruption – that can predictably follow any significant government investigation and prosecution of corporate misconduct. The maintenance of a well-designed and genuinely motivated compliance program is, we submit, the single most important fact available to a company seeking to mitigate the consequences of regulatory foot faults or, in the rarer instances where it occurs, fraud, accounting abuses and criminal malfeasance. Indeed, regulators and enforcement authorities increasingly expect that businesses establish and maintain effective compliance programs and a company that operates without one operates at increased peril of government intervention. It should be no surprise then that the adoption of robust, top-down compliance programs has become a best practice for complex business organizations.

A Hypothetical -- Launching the Corporate Compliance Program, "*Never too Early or too Late*"

Consider the following scenario:

While your company has long had in place a corporate integrity and compliance program, your Genetics Division was acquired without this infrastructure. It had no internal auditor and no in-house counsel – an outside law firm was used by Division management only when absolutely necessary, and then to handle discreet one-off legal issues or to help with transactional work. There had been a lot of consultants and temporary staff hired to manage important business functions. There had also been before and after the acquisition significant turnover in the Division's finance group. Compounding that, the Division still had a very entrepreneurial "feel." Huge pressure existed to meet revenue goals, and financial performance bonuses were lavish, as were other perquisites extended to the company's best performers.

Your acquisition due diligence team had predicted many of the cultural and operational challenges that the Genetics Division would present to your business and had recommended the early integration of the Division into the systems that had well-served your core business. In the months that followed the acquisition you had had several meetings at headquarters with your in-house legal team about how best to roll out the company's Compliance and Corporate Integrity Program to the Genetics Division. There had, however, been a frustrating resistance by Division management to efforts to integrate the Division generally, and a surprising hostility by the Genetics Division CFO to the Compliance Program roll out plan and timetable.

The focus of the pending federal investigation of the Genetics Division over the last few months has become much clearer, as subpoenas demanding documents and data were received and as the company learned of the direction of the government's questioning of company employees. Last week your General Counsel advised you that the company's legal team had concluded with some confidence that the source of the information that had led to the government's investigation more likely than not was a former employee who was still a close friend of one of the Genetics Division billing supervisors. In fact, counsel believed that the government probably had in its possession a federal civil "False Claims Act" whistleblower complaint that had been filed "under seal" by that employee. Counsel explained to you that, as is required by law when private federal 'qui tam' whistleblower law suits are filed, the government is sent a copy of the complaint before it is made public in order to allow the government to evaluate whether to join in the lawsuit. Counsel was concerned that the former employee was not only aware of billing irregularities but had filed a secret qui tam law suit in the hopes of receiving a substantial whistleblower reward from the government.

Yesterday, a review of emails to be produced in response to a grand jury subpoena revealed that one of the Division's three billing supervisors had at least two years before the acquisition tried, without apparent success, to engage the CFO of the Genetics Division (before the acquisition, when it was known as Real Genetics, Inc.) regarding what she had cryptically referred to as "aggressive coding" of Medicare-compensable testing procedures. Your in-house lawyers, hearing this, wanted to redouble the company's efforts to roll out the Compliance Program at the Genetics Division, and to enhance compliance protocols at your corporate headquarters, but you are concerned that those measures would now only look disingenuous, as a form of after the fact 'window dressing' done to mollify the government. Still, something had to be done about the problems at Genetics.

Occasionally the adoption of a corporate integrity program is government mandated. Managed healthcare organizations, for example, are required by federal law to have compliance programs. Government contracts likewise contain express compliance-activity requirements. And, certainly, a company that has been the subject of any significant prior federal investigation or regulatory enforcement action will have been required to adopt such a program. But, otherwise, adoption of a compliance program is completely discretionary.

Where a company has a choice in the matter, it makes abundantly more sense for it to roll out a comprehensive corporate integrity and compliance program before trouble hits than to do so only after bad conduct has revealed itself to the government. Still, even where the impetus is some otherwise unanticipated and calamitous government investigation or regulatory enforcement action, the prompt – and unforced – adoption of a compliance program can go a long way in the eyes of the government towards demonstrating a company's tangible and responsible commitment to remediation.

There exists today an abundance of written guidelines and memoranda – issued by the judiciary and various federal agencies – detailing what federal authorities consider corporate compliance best practice. These materials today guide the efforts of not only companies that have adopted compliance programs but of the many consultants, professionals and other contractors available to help companies roll out compliance measures. There exist many advanced IT solutions as well designed to help with training, reporting and compliance-related communications. The development of these enhanced, cost-effective compliance tools by a burgeoning *compliance industry* has also heightened the expectations of authorities as to the level of compliance activity that should exist – without government prompting – in any complex business organization.

A high-end corporate compliance consultant is likely to address with management a number of common questions:

What are the "*Essential Elements of an Effective Compliance Program*" that regulators and consultants talk about?

Why are these elements laid out most prominently in federal *Sentencing Guidelines*? If a compliance program is truly a forward-looking risk prevention and management undertaking, why are federal *sentencing* authorities and the courts involved in setting compliance standards applicable to day-to-day business operations?

Should a company be concerned that implementation of a compliance program will signal to the government that it believes its employees and managers are not otherwise trustworthy?

What will it take to implement a plan from scratch that will be satisfactory to the government? Are there existing safeguards within the company that it can roll up into a program? Are there recommended "*first steps*"?

Every business organization is different. Is there room in the minds of federal regulators for companies even in the same industry to take markedly different approaches to compliance?

What exactly is a *Code of Conduct*?

How does an "*employee hotline*" work? Will the company be setting itself up by soliciting anonymous complaints that it will then have an implicit responsibility to investigate?

How much is this going to cost the company? What good is it going to do for the company to invest in a compliance program if government agencies and the courts continue financially to reward whistleblowers who take complaints directly to the government?

How best can a company avoid the possible perception – by the government and even by employees – that the program is really just window dressing?

The *"Corporate Compliance Movement"*

The *corporate compliance movement* of the last couple of decades was driven largely by a proliferation of oversized corporate misconduct cases involving allegations of blatant criminal activity. The *Enron, Worldcom* and *Arthur Anderson* scandals of the early 2000s, and the later wave of big dollar and high visibility criminal prosecutions of antitrust, Medicare fraud and Foreign Corrupt Practices Act violations, gave rise to the widespread adoption by most larger and cross-border business organizations of compliance programs designed to root out and quickly fix regulatory and legal transgressions. As executives were sent to prison in increasing numbers and organizational criminal fines rose in magnitude to the $100s of millions, the compliance value proposition became eminently apparent to most.

It comes as a surprise to many that the principal source of guidance available to businesses regarding the best practices attendant to maintaining an effective and robust compliance program is contained in *Sentencing Guidelines* that were promulgated by the United States Sentencing Commission. But the ever-increasing appetite over the last several decades of federal prosecutors and regulators to take on complex business frauds led to the need of the criminal justice system to address in a consistent way when and how severely sometimes seemingly "*victimless*" economic crimes should be prosecuted, punished and remediated. Initially promulgated in 1991, and later enhanced in 2004 after the passage of the Sarbanes Oxley Act, the *Sentencing Guidelines* treatment of what the U.S. Sentencing Commission considered the minimum components of a corporate compliance program sufficient to merit mitigation of organizational sentences filled a void not then addressed anywhere else by statute, rule or industry self-regulation. Since then, and largely because the *essential elements* of an effective compliance program identified there are practical, flexible and easy to understand and communicate, the *Guidelines* have served as the Bible of organizational compliance.

The Necessary Business Predicate – Commitment to the Compliance Proposition

Before launching into the identification of those essential elements, we start with a fact and a definition:

The fact. No matter how enthusiastically a company rolls out a compliance program, and how scrupulously the business follows established training, reporting and accountability protocols, employees are going to misbehave. As long as businesses reward employees monetarily for hitting sales and production targets, and promote those who appear to be better and more clever workers, there will be some element of cheating. While not always criminal, there will always be missteps, dishonesty and wrong-doing no matter the general *good ethics* of an organization

The definition. When we use the term *"compliance"* here, we are not talking about the more routine maintenance of systems to ensure that records are kept in accordance with regulations, that required legal processes or systems are in place, or that certifications and reporting required by law actually occur. Certainly, those sort of compliance activities and processes are important elements of business infrastructure, particularly in regulated industries. What we are referring to in the following pages is more. It is what is needed to deal with the unanticipated mistakes, missteps and bad acts of employees – a compliance program designed to prevent, detect, correct and report affirmative misconduct and to create a culture of lawful behavior through a system that promotes and rewards good behavior while condemning and punishing the bad.

The rolling out of a genuinely undertaken compliance program can easily be sold throughout an enterprise not only as prudent risk reduction but as promoting an organizational culture that values honesty, ethical behavior and basic decency. This will never end up being a hard sell. All manner of positive organizational consequences should flow from genuine and repeated expressions by a company's executive management that the business will be conducted with integrity. And, provided the commitment to compliance is real and not feigned, the adoption of such a program makes it far easier to convince important constituents of the business (and the government) that any subsequent misconduct was the product of errant and rogue employees. As the above chapters make clear, the value of that can be immeasurable.

It all starts, then, with an unflinching institutional commitment – to include buy-in at the highest levels of the organization – to the proposition that honesty and integrity will serve as essential cornerstones of the business enterprise.

The Essential Elements of an Effective Compliance Program

Chapter 8 of the *Sentencing Guidelines* lay out the so-called *"Essential Elements of an Effective Compliance Program."* These elements have become the foundation of the work of an ever-expanding coterie of business and risk management consultants, compliance organizations, accounting and audit professionals and lawyers that advise organizations as to value of adopting what have come to be considered organizational best practices. In the end, the explicit identification in the *Sentencing Guidelines* of the critical components of any effective compliance program very much fuels the expectations of federal regulators and investigators as to how businesses should do their work in this area. The extent to which an organization adopts a program bearing these *"essential elements"* will often directly drive the severity of organizational sentencing recommendations.

The *seven* essential elements of a compliance program are organized around four core objectives:

* The *prevention* of instances of non-compliance in the first instance.
* The prompt *detection* of missteps and misconduct when they occur.
* The *affirmative promotion* of ethical conduct within an organization and the widespread *communication from the top* of an organizational commitment to legal compliance.
* The existence of effective mechanisms to *respond* to instances of non-compliance through *investigation, remediation* and *systems corrections.*

The literature describes the predominant underlying objective of any good compliance initiative as the achievement of an institutional *"culture of compliance"* manifested by organizational components that embrace a true business commitment to legal compliance. As a result, courts, regulators and prosecutors largely reject the adoption of mere *paper* compliance programs and insist instead upon compliance efforts dedicated to fostering a genuine *"tone from the top"* – and *"robust"* – compliance environment.

The *Sentencing Guidelines*, then, identify a series of seven specific components expected to appear in such a program. Those seven *essential elements* feature the clear communication by leadership of compliance, integrity and honesty as core values; the adoption of a statement of organizational values that emphasizes personal and professional integrity; and the implementation of a top-down system of accountability.

Greatly summarized (and annotated), an effective compliance program should:

*   Adopt written standards of conduct and procedures relating to the operation of the organization's compliance program. This is usually addressed through adoption of: (a) a formal written Compliance Program, describing the organization's compliance processes; and (b) an organizational "*Code of Conduct*," detailing expectations regarding employee conduct, reporting and accountability.

*   Designate a person to serve as a Compliance Officer responsible for day-to-day operation of the program with a reporting line to the CEO and the Board. The Chief Compliance Officer should have direct access to the *high level* management responsible for oversight of the program – this access is critical to the ability of senior management to effectively oversee the program.

*   Establish a *compliance committee* at the senior management level responsible for overseeing the compliance program. This required commitment to the involvement of high level personnel is consistent with the admonition that senior management affirmatively "*promote an organizational culture that encourages ethical conduct and a commitment to compliance with the law.*"

*   Implement a training and education regimen both for executive management and for employees.

*   Ensure effective communication between the Compliance Officer and employees. Some organizations set up anonymous hotlines available to employees to call to report misconduct or irregularities. While "*hotlines*" are not necessary for all organizations, there should exist a clear and well understood path upon which an employee can travel to report compliance issues. The system should allow (and affirmatively encourage) employees to "*report or seek guidance … without fear of retaliation.*"

* Enforce standards through well-publicized disciplinary guidelines. A system of accountability should exist, in part through tangible incentives and other organizational recognition of good behaviors, and in part through the consistent imposition of discipline flowing from violations of the Code of Conduct. The success of the program will depend on *compliance accountability* within the organization – making managers truly accountable for failures timely and fully to report compliance lapses and making leadership accountable for the prompt correction of identified problems.

* Monitor, audit, promptly investigate, and self-correct compliance deficiencies. A system should exist wherein the business will "*respond appropriately to [compliance deficiencies, through reviews, investigations and mitigation plans] and to prevent further similar [misconduct], including making any necessary modifications to the organization's compliance and ethics program.*"

Not to belabor the point, what counts most is the *genuineness* of the effort. Efforts that are insincere – the establishment of a *paper* program designed more for optical impression – are easily discerned as such. The government, in assessing the effectiveness of a program, will ask whether employees and managers are appropriately being punished for behavioral lapses and whether good behavior is being rewarded in a way that employees will appreciate, such as though compensation incentive bonuses that factor in the absence of compliance lapses or the employee's positive contributions to ethical behavior. It will ask whether there is a true *top down* commitment to the program – do the CEO and other C-level managers appear to have direct involvement in the effort? Has the company's CEO delivered the right organizational messages? Have sufficient organizational resources been dedicated? Have sometimes difficult to implement systems – like an employee hotline and staff dedicated affirmatively to investigating misconduct – been adopted, or has the company conversely relied largely on out-of-the-box HR training programs and generic admonitions that employees are expected to behave honestly?

Right-Sizing the Compliance Program

While all this can look somewhat rigid in terms of government expectation, the good news is that the *Sentencing Guidelines* say very clearly, and federal authorities well understand, that there is no such thing as a *one size fits all* compliance program. There are few credible off-the-shelf compliance products of universal application. Every organization is of a different flavor, varied in its size, history, complexity, markets, mission, regulatory environment and reporting structure. The *Sentencing Guidelines* say explicitly that compliance programs can and should be tailored to meet those sorts of organizational differences.

Accordingly, federal authorities are not going to expect that a small, intimate organization have as complex a compliance infrastructure as would a larger company. The *Guidelines* set only an expectation that the objectives of an effective compliance program be fairly pursued. How an organization gets there is up to the organization. Factors unique to the organization will dictate the expected elements. So, if a company has had a series of compliance lapses over time or operates in an ethically-challenged business or competitive environment, there will be an expectation of greater formality in the program and rigor in the investigation and punishment of lapses. If due to size the assigned compliance managers are readily accessible to employees and executive management, there will be reduced expectations that the company will employ the sorts of *employee hotlines* used by multi-divisional or geographically dispersed operations, or of the perceived need for the use of formal compliance *dashboards* by company executives to manage the resolution of compliance events.

Even expectations around the detail with which a Code of Conduct – or specific subsections within a larger, more generic Code of Conduct – should be written will vary greatly depending on the operational environment and incumbent compliance risks presented to the organization. A company without unique compliance challenges may set out generally to insist that its employees act honestly, timely report misconduct, cooperate with internal investigations, avoid conflicts of interest or the receipt of other than incidental gifts, meals or entertainment, *etc.* But a company that operates in a sensitive government procurement or regulatory environment will have very detailed sections of a

Code of Conduct dedicated to the avoidance of specifically identified transgressions possible to occur in the industry segment within which the company operates.

"Where Do We Start?"

We suggest that this question – of how a company launches a program entirely from scratch – is easy enough to answer. The company should start simply by picking a Chief Compliance Officer. Not just anyone, but someone with credibility in the organization, someone viewed as a leader. Then the company should task that employee with making recommendations as to next steps. There is an abundance of excellent and easily accessible materials available to educate any newly appointed compliance head and to guide recommendations around the construction of a solid program suitable for even the most complex of organizations.

We do not here mean to be facile. Done right, the adoption of a fully self-standing compliance function will require integration of existing audit, inspection, quality assurance and ethics responsibilities typically assigned to separate managers in most organizations. Organizational changes that will affect existing reporting lines and responsibilities are always challenging and the stuff of organizational change management. The right approach to setting up a compliance program requires some period of initial study and recommendation, and then deliberation by the company's executive management team, leading to an agreed organizational commitment to its success. Selection of a compliance officer appropriately-placed in the organizational hierarchy can serve as the catalyst for the discussions and deliberations to follow.

In turn, and critical to the exercise, the compliance officer needs a strong, executive level sponsor. Many organizations have put its compliance team under the sponsorship and watch of its in-house General Counsel. Others suggest that proper placement of the compliance function should be with the CFO, Chief Operations Officer or the Internal Auditor. The *legal* model provides more opportunity for the use of the attorney-client privilege to preserve the confidentiality of discrete investigations of internal misconduct. The *operational* or *governance* model suggests to some a greater commitment by the organization to compliance as an operational (as opposed to a watchdog) function. Either way, there needs to exist a strong C-level *owner* of the program to serve as the sponsor of the chief compliance officer so as to help guide the company towards construction of the program – and to maneuver around the inevitable rough spots that will be hit when managers perceive the new or expanded function as a threat to turf.

Achieving widespread organizational *buy in* to the compliance function can be difficult. Success or failure of the initiative usually most immediately turns on how effectively the organization's Board and CEO embrace and promote the program.

Which leads to our final topic.

Establishing the Right *"Tone"* . . . *"From the Top"*

Before a regulator or prosecutor will give a company *credit* for having in place a compliance program, the government will gauge whether there has been sufficient attention to the program at the highest levels of the organization. *"Tone from the top"* are the buzz words. The phrase captures well the expectation. It is expected that employees see the Board and the company's C-level team to be genuinely invested in the program. That will mean visible and frequent manifestations of the company's unequivocal commitment to ethical and honest conduct – to include regular executive-level communications promoting the importance of compliance, personal involvement by executives in training employees on compliance issues and even the sacrificing by the company of otherwise productive members of the team who have proven themselves ethically challenged or resistant to the new environment. If it appears that management is only paying lip service to compliance values, the company risks not only not getting positive credit for its actions but of cultivating the resoundingly negative perception by the government (and maybe more worrisome, by employees) that the company is disingenuous about its core values. Accordingly, great care and sensitivity must be had as to internal communications about the launch or effectiveness of any planned compliance program, and the burdens or costs of managing it. Management's orientation towards compliance should always be focused on the fact that it's *"the right thing to do,"* and not that *"the government will give us credit for this thing if we ever need it."*

Bottom line, it is hard to argue against institutionalizing the expectation of personal and organizational integrity. No organization appreciates the need of having in place an effective compliance program more than one that has suddenly and unexpectedly uncovered some significant transgression resulting in intense scrutiny and the potential of substantial negative consequences to the organization, its management and its people. Mistakes will always happen. Taking steps to prevent and detect both innocent missteps and malfeasance (and all the stuff in between) is always a prudent, socially responsible – and cost effective – measure.

About the Contributors

Heber Maughan and **Linda Joy Sullivan** operate a PCAOB-registered, multi-jurisdictional audit and forensic accounting firm, serving clients nationally through their four U.S. offices.

Between his employment with one of the former "Big 4" global accounting firms and the later establishment of his own audit and accounting practice, **Heber Maughan** held senior management posts for public and private companies, to include serving variously as CEO, Chief Financial Officer, V.P. Finance, Controller and Secretary for a number of national and international concerns. **Maughan**, a CPA and holder of a Master's Degree in Accounting, is a member of the AICPA and the Utah Association of Certified Public Accountants.

Linda Joy Sullivan has for close to two decades audited public companies, provided income, estate and trust tax services, prepared complex financial projections, and helped companies meet their SEC financial reporting requirements. She specializes in providing forensic services, to include the handling of tax controversies, serving as an expert witness, conducting investigations and providing litigation support. In addition to being a CPA, she holds an LLM in international Taxation and an MBA. She also today serves as a Representative in the Vermont General Assembly.

Further information about Mr. Maughan, Ms. Sullivan and their firm can be found at *www.maughansullivanllc.com*.